Self-Publish

Like a Pro

Self-Publish Like a Pro

The Step-by-Step Guide To Book Production, Marketing & Global Distribution

Brandie A. Knight

Holley Martin Publishing, LLC • PONCA CITY

Library of Congress Control Number: 2012909147

Publisher's Cataloging-in-Publication Data
Knight, Brandie A.
    Self-publish like a pro : the step-by-step guide to book
production, marketing, & global distribution / Brandie A. Knight.
        p. cm.
    Includes index.
    ISBN: 978-0-9833273-0-1
    1. Self-publishing—United States. 2. Authorship—
Marketing. 3. Books—United States—Marketing. 4. Book
industries and trade.   I. Title.
Z285.5 .K65 2012
070.5—dc23

                                        2012909147

Printed in the United States of America.
First Edition: October 2012

Book Layout & Cover Design by Holley Martin Publishing
Edited by Barbara Pappan

Dedicated to my wonders of the world, Felecia and Dustin, who inherited my business smarts but hold their own on a rare intelligence level.

To a brilliant individual and one-of-a-kind breed, Steve, who compliments my life and stands beside me ready to take on the world.

To Professor Ramon Jones, who challenged me to become the best writer that I can be, thank you.

Special thanks to Fran Kusala and Warren Durso.

ABOUT THE AUTHOR

Brandie A. Knight is a twenty-two year business and marketing veteran. For much of that time, Ms. Knight consulted businesses in the execution of low-cost marketing techniques that deliver high-revenue results. From start-ups to established companies, she has helped businesses understand the processes needed to gain significant revenue growth. In addition to consulting, Ms. Knight owned a public relations firm that catered to a variety of high profile and celebrity clientele, the creator and publisher of lifestyle magazine *Party Chasers*, and a partner in Hollywood Revolutions, a licensing agency for intellectual property. She is currently a classroom instructor, the owner of Holley Martin Publishing, an independent publishing company, and a partner in 100th Monkey Productions, a TV/film production company. Brandie Knight is the author of four books including *The Business Plan Workbook, Self-Publish Like a Pro, Book Marketing Like a Pro*, and her best-selling novel *Hollywood Under the Covers*.

Visit her Website at BrandieKnight.com.

TABLE OF CONTENTS

LIST OF ILLUSTRATIONS

INTRODUCTION

I wrote *Self-Publish Like a Pro* to help inspiring authors reach their dreams of being published in a global marketplace. Achieving success in the publishing arena requires a well-written book, knowledge of the publishing industry, effective marketing, and self-discipline.

The first time you publish your book is exciting, and the sense of accomplishment is overwhelming, especially when book sales soar, and readers take the time to send positive feedback. For most authors, this requires publishing the book on their own. It's an endeavor that requires focus, hard work, and determination in order to succeed. A self-publisher is more than an author; he or she is an entrepreneur who takes on the responsibility of a book's production, marketing, and distribution. This publishing model allows the author complete artistic freedom, 100% control of the copyright, and the highest percentage of the profits.

Self-Publish Like a Pro is a roadmap for authors, who are interested in self-publishing by forming an independent publishing company. Within these pages, you will find essential knowledge about self-publishing in today's world. You will discover how to self-publish through utilizing the same methods implemented by major publishers. The information will help prepare you for a publishing venture that best suits your needs.

You control your own destiny by self-publishing. So, if you have a great book and lots of determination, turn the page to get started on the road to success!

Chapter 1

The Publishing Industry

The knowledge of the publishing industry is important to obtain an over-all understanding of the business and strategically plan your new venture. Since 2009, the publishing industry has experienced significant change to the traditional business model due to the popularity of Internet, digital downloads, and mobile technology. Current market conditions show an extreme decrease in traditional sales, and a significant sales increase for digital products and online retailers.

The publishing industry's current market condition looks grim for sales from the traditional business model. Over the last two years, the publishing industry has been shaken by thousands of physical bookstores closing the doors to business. The nation's second-largest book chain, Borders, went out of business, because they could not compete with Amazon.com and Barnes & Noble, who dominates the online retail book market.

Print books and physical bookstores are in a state of declining sales. In August 2011, the publishing industry's comprehensive survey, BookStats, was released. The study confirmed hardcover, trade paperback, mass market paperback, and audio books on compact discs decreased in sales during 2009 and 2010 and sales for physical retail stores dropped by 42.3 percent. As part of the traditional business model, publishers heavily rely upon these products and sales channels as the core of their business.

The online digital world has changed how books are being marketed and sold. The Internet has become a global way of life, and approximately 1.9 billion people are spending a large percentage of their day online. With popular mobile devices, the Internet can be accessed not only with computers but through cellular phones, e-book readers, and tablets such as iPad and Kindle Fire.

The growing popularity of digital book formats has steadily increased over the last few years. BookStats reported the publishing industry grew in 2009 and 2010, mainly due to over a billion dollars in sales from e-books. In 2010, text-only e-books had an increase of 201.0%, which translates to $863.7 million in sales; enhanced e-books had a 255.1% increase with $14.3 million in sales; digital audio books had a 23.6% increase hitting $124.3 million in sales. In April 2011, the Association of American Publishers reported February 2011 sales resulted in the e-book format ranking number one among all book formats. The report revealed that e-books have grown by 202.3% and digital audio books increased by 36.7% compared to February 2010. In April 2012, Microsoft announced a $300 million investment in the Nook, which is an e-book reader owned by the second largest online bookseller, Barnes & Noble. Microsoft has eliminated the Microsoft Reader and will join forces with Barnes & Noble in the e-book reader market.

The popularity of e-commerce has resulted in the sales of online retailers to soar to new heights. According to BookStats, online retailers experienced an 88.8% increase in book sales between 2008 and 2010. In 2011, Amazon.com, the number one online bookseller, announced that e-book sales in their Kindle store had bypassed print book sales. These figures illustrate that the publishing industry's sales channels have shifted online.

For major publishers, e-books have a low profit margin, and they can not compete with independent publishers and self-published authors, who can sell their e-books at low prices. Publishers have to pay out royalties to the author, wages to employees, production cost, recoup marketing expenses, and they have become accustomed to high profit margins.

The Internet has opened a perfect competition market where independent publishers and self-published authors can finally compete with major publishers. In 2011, Amazon announced John Locke was the first self-published author to sell one million books in their Kindle store, and afterwards, Locke was offered a major publishing deal that he turned down to continue publishing on his own.

A misconception still remains within society where the public believes an author must be published by a major publishing house in order to be considered a "real" writer. Some writers still believe their writing is not validated without a major publisher willing to invest in publishing their manuscript. A certain stigma remains within society about self-publishing that is viewed as a last resort for vain writers who want to see their name in print. Before the Internet became a profitable environment for independent publishers and self-published authors, these statements were closer to the truth. Today, talented authors have willingly and successfully taken the self-publishing path by choice. Several authors have turned down major publishing contracts along the way.

There are several cons to a major publishing contract. Major publishers are making their authors responsible for building and maintaining online platforms for promotional purposes. They put marketing dollars behind one to two books a year. The remaining authors represented by the publisher must self-promote. Publishers obtain creative control over the book's production and promotion. Authors are paid low royalty percentages, and publishers recoup expenses from sales before paying out royalties. Most first-time authors never receive additional money beyond the initial book advancement. The royalty advancement must be paid back to the publisher through future book sales.

The pro to being published by a major publish is "if" the publisher plans to put their marketing dollars behind your book, you eliminate the responsibility of the book's production, distribution, and other labor involved with publishing and promoting a book.

In today's world, the best way to get published by a major publisher is through impressive book sales. High volume book sales will get you on the bestseller's list and attract a publishing deal. The major publisher will be ready to invest promotional dollars in your book, because you already proved there is a market for your book.

Many authors, who have the ability to be entrepreneurs, are bypassing agents and major publishers for the vast benefits of self-publishing. This can be a smart business decision where you have control of your financial freedom, retain ownership of your book's copyright, maintain creative control, and make the most profit. Self-publishing is now affordable within a global market, available to anyone dedicated to the venture and a financially rewarding experience.

Chapter 2

Form a Publishing Company

You will need to form an independent publishing company to receive the full benefits of a publisher and legally separate yourself from your company. An author can self-publish without forming a publishing company, but you need to understand the limitations and risks involved with choosing this path. There are certain formalities involved with legally establishing and operating a business.

Your company's name is an important part of the business. The name should stand alone and not mirror the title or genre of your book. The publishing company should have a unique name that does not use any part of your own name. This allows your publishing company to appear professional and be a separate entity from you as an author.

You should make a list of possible names and narrow down the choices from there. Once you have a handful of choices, you should search the Internet to see if the names are in use by other companies before making your final decision.

A logo is important to your company's identity and for branding purposes. You will need to design a company logo to use on various business materials. A logo can be designed with the company's name and an image incorporated in the design, or just the company's name. The name should be designed by using a specific font and by creating a unique appearance. You should be happy with the logo before you start using it. Once you use the logo, it will establish your company's identity and should not be changed at any point during the lifetime of your publishing company.

Home-based businesses should use an alternative business address for privacy protection. Authors become well-known to their readers and over time develop devoted fans. Both loyal and disgruntled readers can show up at the home of authors. You should plan ahead to protect your privacy. You might consider using a mailbox store or post office box for your established business address.

A mailbox store will provide you with a physical address where you can receive packages via United Parcel Service (UPS), Federal Express (FedEx), and other mail carriers. The physical address will appear as an office location, because mailbox services are located in business districts. The disadvantages are the higher cost for the mailbox service than a post office box, and most companies do not allow mail forwarding when you end the service.

A post office box is a low cost way to establish an alternative business address, and when you end the service your mail can be forwarded to a new address. You can only receive mail from the United States Postal Service (USPS) with a post office box. Your physical home address can be used when you place orders that involve package carriers.

Pricing and service information is available from your local mailbox store and post office. Once you review the information, you can proceed with the service that meets your needs.

A start-up company needs to form a business entity and obtain any required permits to operate within your city, county, state, and federal regulations. Some states provide a start-up business check list on the Secretary of State or Public Regulations Commission Website. Each state is different for who oversees the formation of business entities.

A business entity is the legal structure of a company. There are several types of business entities, but the two most popular for small businesses will be discussed.

A sole proprietorship means an individual owns the company where the owner and business are one in the same. A sole proprietorship does not protect the individual from liabilities such as a lawsuit being brought against the company. If someone sues your publishing company and wins a judgment, your personal assets could be at risk along with your business assets. In most states, the formation of a business entity is not required for a sole proprietorship, but a fictitious name filing needs to be filed. A fictitious name search will be conducted to make sure no other company in the state is operating a business under the same name.

A Limited Liability Company (LLC) can be formed by an individual owner or a partnership. An LLC entity provides the owner with protection from liabilities where the owner is separate from the company. This business entity is appealing for personal protection from liabilities.

When determining the type of business entity to form, you should seek advice from an attorney and/or a certified public accountant (CPA). You can file a business entity without an attorney by acquiring the proper form and following the instructions, but you should seek advice from professionals on the proper business structure that will meet your needs.

Permits may be required for the city or county that you plan to operate your home-based business. You can call your local city and county clerk's office to inquire about this information.

If you plan on selling your book direct to the public for a retail price through your official Website or in-person, you will need to acquire a sales tax permit if there is state sales tax collected in your state. For retail sales, a company is required to charge sales tax to the customer when a product is sold and turn over the sales tax money to the state. You can contact the Sales and Use Tax Division, which is a department with the State Tax Commission, or in some states, it is called the Taxation & Revenue Department. You will be provided with a sales tax chart that provides the tax percentage to charge for retail sales in various areas within your state. If you plan on strictly selling your books through distribution outlets and special sales at wholesale prices, you do not need a sales tax permit.

Obtaining a Federal Identification Number (FIN) allows you to work with the same service providers as the major publishers. The federal government assigns a FIN for business identification purposes, and it is used like a social security number. A free FIN can be acquired for opening a business bank account to avoid using your social security number. The form can be acquired at IRS.gov. You may decide to consult a CPA about this tax matter.

Once you have a company name, address, Articles of Organization for the formation of your business entity, and a Federal Identification Number, you can open a business checking account. You should consider opening an account that offers a debit credit card. This allows you to make important business purchases online or over the phone.

If you plan to sell books through your official Website, you will need to acquire a global payment service like Paypal that allows you to accept global credit cards and other forms of payment. You can receive multiple currencies worldwide for book sales from your official Website. Once you establish an account, there is an option to accept foreign currencies as American dollars. You must set up a Paypal business account not a personal account to operate your publishing company. If you do not plan on selling your book direct to the public, you may acquire a Paypal business account to pay for professional services over the Internet instead of using a bank debit card. For more information, go to PayPal.com.

With certain service providers, you will need to acquire an International Standard Book Number (ISBN). The thirteen digit number identifies the book's title and publisher. The numbers are strictly sold to publishing companies. Major retailers, booksellers, and libraries use bibliographic databases to identify the book and publisher by the ISBN number. Consumers use ISBN numbers to locate books. Distributors and booksellers use it to track inventory and sales. An ISBN is an important tracking device for your book.

R.R. Bowker is the exclusive United States ISBN agency and can be located at ISBN.org. Identifier Services located at MyIdentifiers.com is operated by R.R. Bowker and where you purchase an ISBN. After the online purchase, you will receive an instant ISBN.

The numbers are assigned in quantities of 1, 10, 100, and 1,000. As of the publication date, the cost for one ISBN is $125 for a base package that includes the following: a single ISBN number, account access to update your book information, a free listing in *Books in Print*, SEO Title Card for search engines to provide information about your book, and other resources for publishers. As of the publication date, the cost for a block of 10 ISBN numbers is $250. This breaks down to a cost of $25.00 per ISBN. You do not have to assign a book title to each ISBN at the time of purchase. You are assigned a block of numbers to activate individually when you are ready to publish a new book or various book formats.

Each book format of the same title requires a different ISBN, because each format is considered a different product. A soft cover print version, audio book on compact disc, digital audio book, and each e-book format require a different ISBN for distributors, retailers, and customers to know the exact format that is being purchased.

Before you start assigning the numbers to various book formats, you should read the service provider's guidelines and requirements. For example, Amazon.com supplies Amazon Standard Identification Numbers (ASIN) to e-books submitted through their Kindle Direct Publishing program and to digital audio books submitted to Audible.com.

The ISBN number assigned to your title must be printed on your book's copyright page and on the barcode located on the back cover.

A barcode is a scan code with a book's ISBN used to track inventory and sales by physical retailers and booksellers. It contains your ISBN number to identify the title and publisher within a bookseller's computerized database.

Before you purchase a barcode, you should check with your service provider. Some service providers offer a free barcode for print formats as part of their service. Digital book formats do not use barcodes.

A barcode can contain the retail list price for the book, but this is optional. There are downfalls to displaying a retail price on the barcode. If you make a price change, a graphic artist must update the barcode on the book's cover, and you will be charged a fee for updating the book's file with your service provider. Also, your book sales can be suspended for up to eight weeks once booksellers are notified of the price change. Booksellers know the retail list price when your book is made available for sale, and there is no need to put the price on the barcode.

A company letterhead needs to be designed and can be accomplished by using Microsoft Word, Microsoft Publisher, or a design program. The letterhead should include a company logo, mailing address, company e-mail address, Website address, and phone number. The letterhead design can have all of the information at the top of the page, or your company logo at the top and the remaining information at the bottom.

Chapter 3
Bookkeeping, Order
Fulfillment & Inventory

Bookkeeping is an important aspect of your publishing company. You can take on this task yourself with a bookkeeping program such as Quicken or hire a bookkeeper.

Many businesses take care of their own bookkeeping, which requires entering expenses and revenue into a bookkeeping program and saving the documentation such as receipts. At tax time, these companies hire a CPA to do their business taxes. If you hire a CPA, you will save money by providing a summary of your business expenses and revenue to the CPA. You do not have to provide actual receipts to the CPA, but you do need to save the receipts with the tax paperwork in case of an audit.

Receipts pertaining to your publishing company must be retained for tax purposes. A simple method is to mark two file folders with the following names: "[current year] Expenses" and "[current year] Revenue." When it is time to do the weekly or monthly bookkeeping and annual tax filing, you will have everything in two folders.

Along with keeping your expense receipts for tax deductions, car mileage should be documented for business purposes. You can keep a small notebook in your vehicle to log the business mileage. Every entry should have the following information: the date, destination, the purpose of going to that location, and the mileage. If you mail book orders at the post office, write it in your log book. You will use the log book when you file your business taxes. An alternative to a mileage log book is to use the "directions" function on Mapquest.com that can provide you with an accurate mile count and when printed acts as a receipt of your actual mileage.

For the revenue folder, you will keep all of your direct sales receipts, sales reports from book distributors, and all other income documentation for your company.

Order fulfillment is the process of receiving a product order that involves invoicing, packaging, and shipping. Your book orders can be received from a variety of sources such as special sales, Internet sales, in-person sales, and mail order sales. The order fulfillment process begins when an order is received by a publishing company.

Payment guidelines need to be established for product sales. The requirement of advance payment for book sales is a good idea for a home-based business. When you allow companies to make bulk wholesale purchases on credit, you are putting yourself at risk of not getting paid or tying up your inventory investment waiting to receive payment. Large companies for special sales will usually need an invoice up-front to make a payment in advance.

You will need to make payment exceptions for certain companies such as one of the major library distributors, Quality Books, who require books on consignment. Some large companies involved with special sales may require a thirty or sixty day period before making a payment after they receive the books. The judgment call will be up to you as different circumstances arise for payment arrangements.

For credit accounts, a percentage of interest for late payments should be established along with an effective date that the interest will go into effect. For example, after sixty days, two percent interest per month will be charged to the purchaser. The two percent interest is figured from the total amount due on the invoice. The interest rate can range from one percent to two percent. You will decide the percentage of interest and use the same percent for all credit accounts. Each month, you should send an invoice to the purchaser that reflects the total amount due with the interest rate. This invoice will act as a reminder that the bill is due.

An invoice is an itemized document that lists the products billed to a purchaser with the details of all the costs involved with the transaction. Invoices can be used as a packing slip receipt for advance payments, or a bill to request an advance payment before the books are shipped, or a bill for credit accounts.

Computer generated invoices through a bookkeeping program are the most effective way to create, document, and track multiple invoices. The bookkeeping program can be customized with your book's inventory, and the invoices can be set up with a "quantity shipped" column.

Your running inventory will be adjusted to reflect the amount of books sold when invoices are created within the bookkeeping program.

A bookkeeping program will prompt you to input certain information such as your company's logo, name, address, product details, pricing, and inventory. An invoice template can be created by automatically importing the personalized information from within the program and by customizing the header titles for your specific use as a publishing company. The header titles can include quantity, ISBN number, product description (book's title), list price, discount percentage, and net total.

To prepare an invoice, you will type the needed information on an invoice within the bookkeeping program and print two copies. One copy will be mailed to the purchaser if it is a bill requesting advance payment, and the other copy will be filed in an "open account" file folder. For paid accounts and credit accounts, an invoice serves as a packaging slip inside the shipping box. You will make two copies of the invoice, one for your records and one to include inside the shipping box. For paid accounts, the second invoice will be filed in the "revenue" file folder. For credit accounts, the invoice will be filed in an "open account" file folder.

You will print blank invoices for in-person sales calls for wholesale orders. When you make an in-person sale, you will handwrite two copies. One invoice will be left with the purchaser, and you will keep the other copy for your records. Once you return to the office, you will input the in-person sales invoice in the bookkeeping program.

Single book orders can be shipped in a padded bubble mailer through the United States Postal Service. The media mail is the cheapest way to mail books. The delivery can take a minimum of eight to ten days within the United States and longer for international orders. First class mailing will cost more than media mail, but the envelope arrives quicker to the destination. You can give the customer multiple shipping options such as media mail, first class mail, or priority mail. A single book can usually fit in a priority mail document package.

All international mailings must include a Customs Declaration form that can be acquired at your local post office. The Customs Declaration form is a legal document that states the contents of a package, weight, and the value of the contents.

Bulk book orders can be shipped through the United States Postal Service by using priority boxes with a flat shipping rate. Large bulk orders can be shipped through UPS where the packages are tracked, and the books are automatically insured for a specific amount per box. You can arrange bulk orders to be shipped directly from your commercial book printer to the purchaser and save on shipping cost.

Internet sales through your official Website will mostly be single book orders. Orders received over the Internet will not require you to create and send an invoice to the purchaser. If you are using Paypal, an invoice is automatically prepared for the purchaser. A copy of the invoice is sent to your e-mail account in order to prepare and ship the order. You will need to add the Internet sales invoices in your bookkeeping program to keep an accurate record of sales and running inventory.

In-person sales happen when you are face-to-face with a buyer who places a wholesale order, and you fill the book order on-the-spot by delivering the books, writing an invoice, and collecting money for the transaction. Bulk orders for specialty stores are considered in-person sales.

Single orders for after lectures and seminars are in-person sales, but this type of sale does not require an invoice. Before the in-person event, you will count your book inventory and do a recount after the event. The number of books sold will be entered into your bookkeeping program.

Mail order sales can be received through snail mail or e-mail. The mail orders can result from special sales order forms contained inside your sales kit.

Bookstore orders should go through distributors due to the risk of the stores going out of business before you receive payment for your books. The exception will be local bookstores that you have made special arrangements with for leaving your books on consignment or direct sales.

Your service providers will take care of the order fulfillment as part of their service, and you will be provided with publisher's compensation reports that detail your monthly book sales.

A file folder named "Complimentary Books" is a good idea to keep track of inventory loss. A print format and audio book on compact disc are the company's products that are being printed, purchased, and resold at a markup price. When you place an order for books, it becomes inventory. The running inventory throughout the year changes every time you purchase new books, sell books, and giveaway books. All of the inventory must be accounted for during the year. On a business tax return, you will provide the starting inventory for the tax year and provide an amount of inventory loss for the year.

You can generate an invoice for each complimentary book that in-cludes giveaways for promotional purposes, book reviews, legal registra-tions, and professionals who helped with the production. Note on the invoice the reason for the complimentary book and a zero amount owed. This will adjust the inventory and help keep an accurate record. You will print two invoices. Place one invoice in the complimentary book file and the other you will use as a packing slip.

Chapter 4
The Marketing Mix

Product, price, distribution (place), and promotion are the elements known as the marketing mix. Each element is an ingredient that is mixed together in a specific way to attract and meet the needs of customers. A strategic marketing mix is the foundation for a successful business and should create a competitive advantage for the publisher.

As a publisher, your book is the product, and there are different book formats that can be offered as part of your product line. You need to decide what formats will be offered by your company such as print books (print-on-demand), e-books, enhanced e-books, and audio books.

Print-on-demand (POD) is a non-inventory model where books are printed to meet the demand of the market. POD books are printed when an order is placed for retail or wholesale, and directly shipped to the buyer from the POD service provider. One book or a thousand books can be printed for the same cost to the publisher. This concept is a money-saving breakthrough for independent publishers.

Several print-on-demand service providers supply an ISBN as part of their service, and some providers require you to have your own ISBN. If you use the POD service provider's ISBN, your book will show up as being listed under the service provider's publishing company, and there will be no need to buy an ISBN. Using your own ISBN will greatly benefit your publishing company and help with marketing your book.

Commercial book printers charge by the quantity of books to be printed in a single print run. The higher quantity of books will equal a lower cost per book. Most self-publishers do not have the start-up capital to order a thousand books or have an adequate place to store the inventory.

The print version of your book can be printed by a commercial book printer, POD service provider, or both. Most authors will end up using both depending on their needs for a small or large print run. Most POD service providers do not offer high volume print runs.

Once your company gets into high volume orders from special sales, you will need to locate a commercial book printer for large print runs. You can make arrangements with a commercial printer to print the books, use your company's information on the shipping labels, and ship the high volume orders directly to your customers.

An e-book is a digital formatted file that can be downloaded and read on devices such as computers, cellular phones, e-book readers, and tablets with Internet capabilities. With mobile technology increasing in popularity, e-books are capturing a growing percentage of book sales. Some authors are bypassing print versions and focusing on e-books due to the fast production time and low production cost.

An e-book has a low production cost that involves an interior layout that is different from the print format, front book cover design (the spine and back cover are eliminated), and an e-book file conversion. An e-book conversion is a book's computer file that is transferred into a designated file format that allows the e-book to be read on a specific digital device. Once the initial production is complete, you can sell the same digital file unlimited times without recurring production or printing costs.

The e-book service provider should have a digital fulfillment system that involves digital rights management and secure content delivery. Digital rights management is restriction controls that prevent the unwanted access to copying, converting, sharing, or distributing the e-book's digital content by the consumer. Secure content delivery is a protective system where only the paying customer has access to downloading the e-book.

There are several e-book conversion formats available for different reading devices. You can make available all of the e-book versions or pick certain formats for your product line.

An enhanced e-book is a multimedia, digital book that includes additions to the original content of a book such as video, audio, images, and interactivity. A publisher can offer supplemental materials to enhance the reader's experience.

Enhanced e-books offer added value to the consumer. The production cost and licensing rights to use copyrighted material such as music, photos, and videos can be expensive. If these items are created in-house where the publisher or author owns the copyright, the production cost is much lower. Another way to cut costs is to make arrangements with copyright holders to use their material for free as a way to promote their artistic work or use free public domain items.

There are two types of audio books: digital audio file for downloading and compact disc (CD). Few audio books are being published by independent publishers and self-published authors due to what is perceived as an expensive production cost. Many people believe that you have to use a professional studio and voiceover talent that involves steep hourly rates to record an audio book, but this is not true. Audio computer software can be utilized to record audio books at a low cost. After the initial production, there are no reoccurring costs involved for a digital audio book, and the digital file can be resold unlimited times. You will encounter reoccurring printing costs for audio books on compact discs.

The major publishers, who are distributing audio books, are making a high profit margin. More independent publishers need to offer audio books to drive the retail price down. This is a prime market to get noticed by offering digital audio books at low prices.

There is growing popularity with audio books for consumers with active lifestyles. Truck drivers, traveling salesmen, and people who spend many hours in their vehicles are listening to audio books. People listen to audio books on their mobile devices while exercising, commuting, and mowing the yard. By offering an audio version of your book, you will generate extra revenue from tapping into the audio group of consumers.

You may decide simply to publish e-books and digital audio books. Many authors have been very successful with this approach. Although the digital book formats are soaring in popularity, there are still people who prefer the print format of a book and the audio book on compact disc.

By the time you finish reading this guide, you should have a complete understanding of the benefits to offering the different book formats, and you can make an informed decision about what formats will meet the needs of your potential readers.

The price is an important aspect that determines how well your book will sell to wholesale distributors and in the retail marketplace. A publisher sets the wholesale discount price and the retail list price for each book format that will be made available in the market.

In the publishing industry, there is a standard 55% wholesale discount for booksellers. This discount allows booksellers a competitive margin to offer a sale price to their customers. The retail price set by booksellers does not affect the publisher, who still receives the same wholesale price per book. If a standard 55% wholesale discount is not offered, it will severely limit the number of distribution avenues available to the publisher.

You will need to research books of similar genre and page count to compare the retail list prices set by other publishers. Amazon.com has the retail price listed and usually the price is slashed through to show a discounted sale price. You will need to make sure you are working off of the retail price and not the sale price.

> ### Standard 55% Wholesale Discount
>
> For example, after researching retail prices, you decide $24.95 is a fair retail price for your print format.
>
> Next, you should calculate the numbers to see if you are happy with the profit margin.
>
> To calculate a price, you will enter $24.95 in the calculator and multiply it by 55%, which equals $13.72.
>
> Now, enter $24.95 and subtract $13.72, which equals $11.23.
>
> The wholesale price for your book is $11.23 for distributors.

The wholesale price increases with every middleman distributor, and the 55% wholesale discount margin decreases for wholesale book buyers who purchase through a middleman distributor. For example, let's say that you are using Lightning Source, Inc (LSI) as your POD service provider. Amazon.com and BarnesAndNoble.com buy print formats directly from LSI without a middleman, and they get to take full advantage of the 55% discount. In order to entice buyers, they can put a book on sale at various price points. They decide how much their profit margin will be by discounting the retail price. They are cutting into their profit margin, not the publishers. You will receive the same profit per book, because your cut comes out of the wholesale price minus the printing cost.

After you have secured service providers and have estimated number of finished book pages, you will need to figure out the average cost per unit. This information provides the cost and profit for each product.

Average Cost & Profit Per Unit

For example, you take the wholesale price of $11.23 and subtract the printing and shipping cost of $5.63 for a book with 364 pages, which equals $5.60. Your publisher's compensation is $5.60 per book.

The following is an example of an average cost and profit form.

Print Format (POD) Finished Size: 6 x 9

Page Count: 364

Interior: Black and White

Retail List Price: $24.95

Wholesale Discount Price: $11.23

Profit Per Unit: $5.60

Average Cost Per Unit: $5.63

An audio book on compact disc would be figured the same as the previous example, but the page count will be replaced with the time length of the audio book.

The e-book retail list price is figured the same way as the print format without the printing cost. Some e-book service providers will purchase the digital content at the wholesale discount price from the publisher. Other service providers offer a royalty rate to the publisher, and the percentage the service provider retains covers digital rights management and content delivery as well as a profit margin.

The highest royalty rate offered to publishers is for Kindle e-books at Amazon.com, which Amazon holds the greatest market share for e-book sales. Kindle Direct Publishing (KDP) offers a seventy percent royalty option. As of the publication date, in order to qualify for the 70% royalty, your Kindle e-book must be priced between $2.99 and $9.99. In order to receive the new royalty in other countries as it comes available, you must have the worldwide rights available within your Amazon KDP account.

There are no cost per unit for e-books, enhanced e-books, and digital audio books after the initial production cost, but you still need to figure out your profit per unit with each service provider.

E-book Profit Per Unit

Amazon Kindle E-book

Retail List Price: $9.95

Profit Per Unit: $6.97

Average Cost Per Unit: $0

The example below would be the low end of Amazon's 70% royalty rate.

Amazon Kindle E-book

Retail List Price: $2.99

Profit Per Unit: $2.05

Average Cost Per Unit: $0

Distribution is the place your book formats will be made available for purchase by consumers. A distribution channel is an organized process to facilitate the movement of a book from the publisher to wholesalers and booksellers until the product reaches the retail consumer.

For the POD service, a publisher must submit camera-ready files according to the service provider's guidelines for the book interior and book cover. Camera-ready is a file that is ready for professional printing as is with no further changes. E-book and digital audio book files work the same way and must be prepared and ready for distribution. Some service providers offer the book production services for a fee.

When choosing POD, e-book, enhanced e-book, or audio book service providers, you will want to inquire about their distribution partners. Ingram is the largest wholesale book distributor in the world with 30,000 distribution outlets in over 100 countries. Wholesale book distributors like Ingram and Baker & Taylor, who the major publishers are distributed through, sell to wholesalers, bookstores, libraries, and retailers. They do not sell direct to the public.

In the past, self-publishers have faced the disappointment of not having access to distribution outlets used by major publishers. As a result of this issue, many authors have turned to service providers called vanity presses and subsidy publishers. A vanity press is a company who charges an author to publish a book and mainly profits from the fees charged to the author. A subsidy publisher is a company who charges an author to print a book under the in-house publisher's imprint using their own ISBN, retains copyright ownership of the author's book, and pays low royalties to the author.

There are several drawbacks to using a vanity press or subsidy publisher. The publisher's imprint is printed on every book that carries a certain level of stigma within the publishing industry. Professional book reviewers will not review these books, and you will have a hard time being taken seriously by the media when seeking publicity. Books published by these companies have an extremely low success rate.

Since subsidy publishers take the copyright ownership of an author's book, this usually is not an acceptable trade-off. Some authors have signed the agreement without realizing that their book's copyright will remain the property of the company.

Before entering into a service agreement, you should fully understand the terms that you are agreeing to, and you may need to consult an attorney for a clear understanding of the legal terminology.

When a publisher seeks distribution services through any company, a service agreement is required. You will need to pay close attention to the agreement. The service agreement will be a non-exclusive agreement, which means you can distribute your book through other companies. You can sell the book on your official Website, through local specialty stores, libraries, and other distribution outlets. An exclusive agreement will limit your distribution with the specific book format. You should make sure the termination clause spells out an easy process for the publisher to end the agreement at any time.

By forming an independent publishing company, you cut out the middleman by going directly to one of the main service providers, Lightning

Source, Inc., (LSI). Companies such as Xlibris, iUniverse, and AuthorHouse use LSI as their service provider, which makes them the middlemen. Their customers pay prices that have been marked up for profit, because these companies make money by providing publishing services. LSI only deals with publishing companies. Authors, who wish to self-publish with global distribution without forming a publishing company, must use a middleman.

LSI has changed the publishing world by offering unmatched services. Ingram Content Group owns LSI, and Ingram is the largest book wholesaler in the country. Books carried by LSI are available in Ingram's electronic catalog, but this is just the beginning of LSI's distribution partners. For more information, go to LightningSource.com.

There are many advantages to using the POD service through LSI, which is not a vanity press or subsidy publisher. As a publisher, you are simply hiring LSI for a professional service. You are an independent publisher, who retains 100% of the copyright ownership of your book. You set the retail list price, wholesale price, and royalty for your publisher's compensation. LSI does not sell direct to the public. They fill orders that come from their distribution partners and from the publisher of the book.

The top two online booksellers in the United States are Amazon.com and BarnesAndNoble.com, which distributes both print and e-book formats. If you use LSI, your print format will be made available on both of these sites. LSI distributes various e-book formats, which is a separate distribution agreement. If you decide to use LSI e-book distribution, you should not submit Kindle, Nook, or iBookstore e-book formats for distribution. You will make a bigger profit by directly signing up for e-book publisher accounts with Amazon's Kindle Direct Publishing, Barnes and Noble's PubIt!, and Apple's iBookstore.

Amazon has worldwide retail distribution with six Websites in various countries and languages. If you make your e-book available for worldwide distribution, the book will be distributed on these sites in English. You can self-publish with Amazon in many languages such as English, French, Spanish, German, Italian, and Portuguese.

There are two ways to distribute e-books on Amazon through non-exclusive and exclusive service agreements located at https://KDP.Amazon.com. E-books can be distributed through Amazon's Kindle Direct Publishing with a non-exclusive service agreement. E-books from the Kindle store can be viewed on Kindle devices, android-based devices, and Kindle apps for PC, Mac, iPad, iPhone, iPod Touch, and Blackberry. If you sign up for an additional program called KDP Select, the e-book agreement is an exclusive distribution service. You are not allowed to distribute your e-book with another service provider during that time period.

KDP Select program is designed to distribute e-books for authors and publisher under a ninety-day exclusive contract, which can be automatically terminated or renewed at the end of the ninety-day period. If Amazon's compliance team finds your e-book selling at other locations, your contract will be terminated. There are several benefits for authors and publishers who participate in this Amazon program.

Your e-book will be available for free to Amazon Prime members through the Kindle Owner's Lending Library. A Prime member receives a free e-book once a month through Amazon's library. However, authors are paid for e-books borrowed from the library from a profit sharing royalty fund that Amazon establishes each month. The royalty sharing pool is calculated with a specific formula that Amazon has established. For April 2012, authors received a royalty rate of $2.48 per e-book borrowed. Authors, who sell their e-books for $2.99 or less on Amazon, made a higher royalty rate with this library lending program than their regular royalty percentage. The royalty rate varies from month-to-month due to how much money is placed in the monthly royalty sharing fund and how many books were borrowed. For April 2012, the royalty sharing fund was $600,000. Since this program has been in place, the royalty rates have increased each month. This program provides authors with another sales avenue to tap into for their e-books.

The KDP Select program offers a free e-book promotion. During every ninety-day contract term, a five day free promotion is available to the author. For five days, the author can make his/her e-book available for free to everyone who shops on Amazon. Giving your e-book away for free may not sound appealing to you, but there are advantages to this promotion. The e-book receives exposure by appearing on the free e-book list. Every time someone downloads the book for free, the e-book rises on the ranking list, and your book could find its way on the top 100 "free Kindle store" bestseller's list. If an author has more than one book available and readers like the free e-book, readers will purchase the other books by the same author. As a result of this promotion, authors can acquire more loyal readers and receive more book reviews. After the five day promotion ends, the e-book moves from the "free" e-book list to the "paid" list. Within a short period of time, the e-book sales can increase, and you could start selling more books than before the promotion.

BarnesAndNoble.com has a non-exclusive service agreement for their publishing program called PubIt! located at PubIt.BarnesAndNoble.com. E-books from the eBookstore can be viewed on Nook readers, and Nook apps for PC, Mac, android, iPad, iPhone, and iPod Touch. The program offers optional features such as Read In Store, Lend Me, and Samples. Read In Store feature offers Nook customers the chance to browse inside e-books for an hour at no charge. Lend Me offers Nook customers the chance to loan an e-book for fourteen days to another person. Samples feature offers customers a chance to read five percent of an e-book before making a final buying decision.

Barnes and Noble's Nook First program is an exclusive thirty-day service agreement with PubIt! members designed to help launch new, unpublished e-books. For e-books accepted into this program, Barnes and Noble will promote the book on their storefront and Nook First page as well as in e-mail campaigns. As a result of this exclusive program, Nook owners are the first to read new e-books. After the thirty-day period, the e-book can be distributed in the marketplace by other distributors.

Apple's iTunes Connect distributes e-books, Multi-Touch books (enhanced e-books) for iPad, and audio books through iTunes and iBookstore. Self-publishers can sign up for this non-exclusive program at Apple.com/itunes/sellcontent. As of June 2011, iTunes had 225 million account holders. iTunes can be accessed on Apple products and computers.

For audio books and e-books, several major publishers use the digital content distributor, OverDrive.com and Amazon's Audible.com. As of the publication date, OverDrive.com and Audible.com distribution requires the publisher to have a minimum of five digital products. You can build your title (book) catalog to use these distributors in the future.

Audiobook Creation Exchange (ACX.com), a subsidiary company of Amazon, provides a distribution service for getting an audio book distributed on Audible.com, Amazon, and iTunes. You can pursue digital audio book distribution through iTunes without a third-party company.

When choosing the right service providers to meet your needs, you should carefully read over the fees and service agreements.

Chapter 5
Financial Planning

An important step for a start-up business is financial planning. You need to know how much it is going to cost to publish your first book.

Start-up capital is a specific amount of money needed to launch your business and get product into the market. You will need a finished manuscript, computer, Internet access, and start-up capital to operate your publishing company.

During the start-up phase of your publishing company, it is important to use personal resources that will save you money. Personal resources are friends, family members, and your knowledge of different tasks that need to be accomplished. As long as the result is quality work, you can use your resources for all of the steps that are discussed. If resources for certain tasks do not exist, you should consider hiring a freelancer at Odesk.com or a professional company to do the job. Another alternative to hiring a professional is to locate an instructional video on YouTube. com that teaches you how to do certain tasks. The key to running a successful business is to maintain a low overhead to achieve a greater profit.

The projected start-up expenses will help you get an overview of how much money is needed to get your book published. Projected expenses mean the figures are accurate to the best of your knowledge. The figures may fluctuate up or down due to unforeseen costs or from an over-estimation of expenses. By preparing the projected start-up expenses, you will discover the total start-up cost and how the money will be spent.

After a list of expense items are compiled, you will need to acquire quotes from the companies that you plan on doing business with for the book production. Do not include items that you can do yourself or free labor from personal resources.

The following is an example of projected start-up expenses for forming a publishing company and production costs for print and e-book formats.

> **Projected Start-up Expenses: Print & E-book**
>
> Equipment: Computer, software programs, etc $0
>
> Legal fees: Business entity, permits, or licenses $125
>
> Registration fees: Copyright registration $35
>
> Book Production: ISBN, P-CIP, copy editor, production design, catalog fee, title set up fee, proofing fee, and e-book conversion $1,557
>
> Office supplies: Printer paper and toner, file folders, and business checks $115
>
> Total Start-up Cost: $1,832.

This example uses sample figures. Your start-up cost may be lower or higher. The cost will be determined by your personal resources where you can save money and the type of book formats you publish.

The entire amount of the start-up capital is not needed up front. The operational stages have certain tasks that need to be accomplished in a specific order. Some tasks require money while other tasks require your time. Once you start generating prepublication orders, the revenue can cover some of the start-up costs.

Your first book will be the most expensive to publish due to forming the publishing company, one-time expenses that are not reoccurring, and a learning curve. Your second book will cost you a fraction of the price.

An alternative option with a low start-up cost is to publish your e-book first on Amazon.com. This approach eliminates the higher start-up expenses involved with the production costs of other book formats. For example, Amazon's Kindle Direct Publishing program assigns the e-book an ASIN, which eliminates the purchase of an ISBN and saves you money on other expenses. You may decide to proceed with this option and gradually expand your book formats when the profits start generating from your e-book sales.

The following is an example of a projected start-up expense form for forming a publishing company and production costs for an e-book distributed on Amazon. The expenses do not include copy editing fee.

> **Projected Start-up Expenses: E-book**
>
> Legal fees: Business entity, permits, or licenses $100
>
> Book production: Cover design, interior layout, e-book file conversion $250.
>
> Total Start-up Cost: $375

Money goals can be set for a financial overview of the start-up capital. Once you are finished reading this book and have followed along with the planning stages, you should examine the projected start-up expenses. On a calendar, you should note the amount of money needed and the name of the expense on specific dates. This will help you visualize your money goals. If you do not meet your money goal by the specific date, you can always move the date. The beauty of starting your own publishing company is you are not restrained by anyone's time schedule but your own.

KickStarter.com can be utilized for raising money to publish your book in various formats or fund your book tour, but it can not be used to form your publishing company. Kickstarter is a funding platform where artists display their creative projects and people help fund the venture by receiving rewards in return. Publishing is one of the artistic categories allowed for project funding. If you do not reach your money goal for the project, Kickstarter has an all or nothing policy where no money or rewards will be exchanged.

You will need certain items to launch a project on Kickstarter. An important aspect is to identify the total amount of money needed to complete your project. Next, you will need to set the amount of time your project will be available for funding such as thirty days or sixty days. Rewards entice people to fund your project. The rewards structure should be at different donation levels such as a fifty-dollar donation will receive fewer rewards than a five-hundred-dollar donation. Rewards can consist of an autographed book, an invitation to your book party, and an exclusive dinner with you (travel expenses not included). You can be creative with the rewards as long as it fits within the guidelines of the program. You will need to make an informative video and provide other pertinent information and images about the project. For more information and project guidelines, you can visit KickStarter.com.

The break-even point is a specific amount of book sales where you have successfully recovered your start-up investment. From the first example, we know the start-up cost is $1,832. The break-even point will happen once the profit reaches that number.

To figure a break-even point with the quantity of books that you need to sell, you will take the profit per unit from, the average cost per unit form, and the total start-up cost from the projected start-up expenses form. Divide the profit per unit into the total start-up cost to find your break-even point.

Break-even Point for POD

Print Format (POD)

Profit Per Unit: $5.60

Total Start-up Cost: $1,832

$1,832 divided by $5.60 = 327.1

Break-even Point: 327 books

Break-even Point for E-book

Profit Per Unit: $6.97

Total Start-up Cost: $1,832

$1,832 divided by $6.97 = 262.8

Break-even Point: 263 books

Your break-even point may be lower or higher. The figure will vary depending on your profit per unit and total start-up cost.

The break-even point will realistically be a combination of profits from the entire product line.

As the revenue starts flowing into your publishing company, it will become working capital to continue operating your business.

Chapter 6
Special Sales

———————————————————

Special sales are opportunities to sell a book in bulk through avenues that do not include booksellers. The profits per book are lower with bulk sales, but the overall profit is higher for single bulk orders.

A sales kit is an informative packet about a new product that contains sales literature and promotional materials. Before you can approach special sales opportunities, you will need to put together a sales kit that includes a business card, sell sheet, price sheet, and cover letter. The contents of a sales kit are placed in a folder for a professional appearance or a compressed file for e-mailing.

You may decide to hire a graphic artist to design the kit, or you can design the materials yourself if you can produce a professional design.

A sell sheet is a sales tool that conveys the most relevant information about your book by using a quick and to-the-point approach. The information should be brief and straight forward. The layout design should be in an easy-to-read format and can use bullet points to get the book's benefits across to the wholesale buyer. You do not want a page full of words, but an attractive design that can be skimmed over by a busy buyer. The sell sheet can be designed as a brochure or flyer, and the appearance is more attractive in color over a black and white design.

The title of your book should be in bold type near the top of the page. The following information can be grouped together: the author's name, genre classification, number of pages, binding type, finished size, retail list price, ISBN, and relevant content. For nonfiction books, the relevant content notes if the book contains the following: glossary, index, bibliography, or illustrations. The relevant content is important to certain buyers like libraries and schools.

The next grouping of text will be the contact information for the publisher that includes the publishing company's name, address, phone number, and e-mail address.

The author's short biography should be included with a header that reads "About the Author."

The book's benefits should appear in a bullet point format next to the front cover image of the book. If the book is fiction or creative nonfiction, a short book description should appear next to the cover image.

The book's wholesale price structure should offer quantity discounts. A quantity discount is an incentive offered to a buyer to receive a cheaper price per unit for purchasing a greater quantity of books. When companies purchase products, they expect a price break per unit for the higher product volume that they order.

Your POD service provider can inform you of how many books will come in a case. For example, 6x9 book with a one inch spine can come in a case of 22 books. Once you get into volume orders over 1000 books, you will be able to get a good price per unit from a commercial printer.

The following is an example of a quantity discount price structure. The discount is taken from the $24.95 retail list price for the print format. The price per unit is the wholesale price that the book is sold for to the buyer. According to the structure below, the minimum quantity of books that a buyer can purchase is twelve.

Quantity Discount Price Structure

Quantity	Discount	Price Per Unit
12 to 44 units	44%	$13.97
45 to 66 units	46%	$13.47
67 to 88 units	48%	$12.97
89 to 110 units	50%	$12.48
111 to 154 units	52%	$11.97
155 to 265 units	55%	$11.23
266 to 815 units	60%	$9.98
816 to 1,541 units	65%	$8.73
1,542 to 2,509 units	70%	$7.48
2,510 + units	75%	$6.24

You may prefer to set up your price structure by cases instead of individual units. The way you set up the price structure is up to you.

Extra promotional materials can be included in the sales kit such as book review quotes or favorable media clippings.

If you are mailing or e-mailing the sales kit to a company instead of an in-person meeting, you will include a personalized cover letter to the buyer. The cover letter should be printed on your company letterhead. In the cover letter, you should briefly introduce your book, why you feel your product is a good fit for their company, and how selling or giving away the product can benefit their business.

A folder is a good idea for the kit to keep the items organized and wrinkle-free. The folder helps keep the items together once the package is opened and placed on the buyer's desk. Do not staple, hole-punch, or paperclip any items in your sales kit. The solid color folders with two pockets and the business card slot on the inside pocket work well.

You can design a custom label to go on the front of the folder with the front cover image of your book or company logo. The large shipping labels that measure 3.25" by 4" by Avery work well and can be purchased at your local office supply store. The label sheets are made to feed into your printer. Once the labels are designed, you can print out a few sheets and keep them in a file folder where the labels are ready-to-use.

Specialty stores are retail stores that specialize in selling theme products such as gardening, hobbies, seasonal, children, construction, and sporting goods. Specialty stores have had success with carrying books that relate to their business and appeal to their customers.

A book about staying fit through exercise and nutrition could be sold through sporting good stores, health food stores, and even gyms that have gift shops. A Christmas storybook for children could be sold through children's clothing stores, seasonal Christmas stores, and toy stores. A book about remodeling kitchens and bathrooms could be sold to construction supply stores, home improvement stores, kitchen and bath stores, floor title stores and counter top stores. Fiction books can be sold to specialty stores that attract customers interested in characters' occupations, book's genre, and the location setting.

You can make a list of specialty stores that are appropriate to target for your book's topic. Your list can include locally owned businesses, regional chains, and national chains as long as the locations are specialty stores.

In-store promotional materials are a way to draw attention to the product and boost book sales. The promotional materials consist of posters, postcards, and point-of-purchase floor and counter displays. These items will be used in the store where your book is available to purchase.

The layout design for the poster and postcard are the same, but the design sizes are different for printing purposes. The finished poster size should be about 17¼ inches tall by 11¼ inches wide. The postcard should be about 5½ inches tall by 4¼ inches wide. The design layout should consist of the book's front cover image. The text should highlight the book's benefits and use a call-to-action such as "Purchase your copy today!"

The posters will be hung around the store. Postcards will be placed next to the checkout registers for customers to pick up if they are interested in your book. You can ask if the postcards could be placed inside the customers' shopping bags.

The point-of-purchase book display can be designed similar to the poster and postcards. The floor display has a header and base design area, and the counter display has a header design area. You will need to know how many books it takes to fill both displays, but the width of your book's spine can not be determined until the interior layout is finished. For example, the three-pocket floor display for 6x9 books has a six inch pocket depth. Twelve books will fit in each pocket for a book with a half inch spine. Twelve books multiplied by three pockets equal thirty-six books.

Once you have your printed books, promotional materials, and sales kit, you are ready to approach the specialty stores on your list. You will approach the local specialty stores with an in-person meeting. For regional and national chain stores, you will need to contact the retail buyer of products for each company.

The local market should be tested first due to limited start-up capital and to grow your business with a logical progression. Once you are successful with selling books in the local stores, you can branch out on a regional and national level.

For the local stores, you will become a traveling salesman for a few days. The planned stops should be mapped out before you leave your office. Once you are at a location, you will ask to speak with the store manager and have your book and sales kit in your hand. If the manager is not available, you will write down the manager's name, find out the best time to reach the person, and leave behind a business card.

If the manager is available, you will go into a sales pitch about being a local author who has written a book. You will explain how your book would be of interest to the store's customers and the book's benefits. The store will want to know their benefits for carrying the product before making a buying decision. A good profit margin and carrying a product that will satisfy their customers' needs are the beneficial selling points. Present the manager with the price sheet, be confident, and speak as if the manager has already decided to make the purchase. You can say something like "I will have the floor display set up in less than five minutes for your customers to start purchasing the book." If the manager is not confident the books will sell, you can offer to leave the books on consignment. You will need to fill out an invoice receipt to document the transaction.

When you successfully make a sell, you should leave your business card for the manager to contact you about restocking the display. You will need to check on the display if the manager does not contact you within a reasonable amount of time.

Universities, colleges, or vocational technology centers might be able to use your book as a textbook adoption. Nonfiction and books of literature might interest university and college instructors, who can use the book as secondary reading requirement in their classes. Vocational instructors might be able to use your nonfiction how-to or instructional manual as a textbook for their classes. Some instructors are not using textbooks to teach the classes and could benefit from your instructional book. The instructor can make arrangements with the school to use your book as a mandatory textbook for students attending the class.

You will need to locate and contact the individual instructors to make an inquiry about textbook adoption. Class schedules are available from the schools to find the appropriate classes that would fit with your book's topic. You can contact school libraries to carry your book.

Some publishers have not figured out a satisfactory business model for how to deal with library sales for e-books. There is a current e-book debate between publishers and libraries. Publishers want to limit the amount of times an e-book can be borrowed from a library before the library must renew the rights to continue distributing the e-book. The library allows an e-book to be downloaded directly from their Website, and publishers feel it will turn e-book buyers into e-book borrowers. Libraries want to offer e-books due to the high demand from their consumers, but they claim the e-book structure is too expensive.

Libraries can be a profitable avenue for book sales, but you need to decide which book formats will be made available, if any, to the library market. Libraries purchase print formats, audio books on compact disc, e-books, and digital audio books. There are numerous public libraries with annual spending budgets to purchase new books.

For a book to be considered for library sales, a Library of Congress Control Number (LCCN) needs to be assigned to the book. A LCCN is the identification of a numbering system created for a book's library catalog record. Libraries use the LCCN to locate a book's bibliographic record and important information within national databases.

The Library of Congress Cataloging in Publication Division offers a free LCCN Pre-assigned Control Number (PCN) program where you can obtain a LCCN for prepublication use, which you will need if you want to acquire book sales from libraries. The Website is located at PCN.Loc.Gov and the process usually takes about one to two weeks.

The LCCN is placed on the copyright page in the front matter of your book. As instructed by the Library of Congress, you will mail the first print copy of your book to the Library of Congress in order to complete your application.

A Publishers Cataloging in Publication (P-CIP) is a block of cataloging data that relates to the book's content. The P-CIP is prepared by a cataloging agent during a book's production stage. The P-CIP block received from this process will be printed on the copyright page in the front matter of a book. Librarians use this data to determine how to catalog a book and where it should be located within the library.

The Library of Congress has a Cataloging in Publication (CIP) program to prepare the cataloging for publishers, but your publishing company must have published books by at least three different authors to be eligible for this program.

Independent publishers can hire a cataloging agent to do a Publishers Cataloging in Publication (P-CIP) such as Five Rainbows Services for authors and publishers located at FiveRainbows.com or Quality Books located at Quality-Books.com. The cataloging agent's guidelines will provide the specific requirements. You will need an ISBN and LCCN before you can acquire the P-CIP.

A book review in the *Library Journal*, a trade publication for libraries, is helpful for capturing the attention of librarians. The *Library Journal* does prepublication reviews and prefers to receive the book three to four months before the publication date.

There are three main book wholesalers that specialize in the library distribution for various formats: Baker & Taylor, Quality Books, and Over-Drive. You can save a lot of time by securing a library distributor with a professional sales force.

Baker & Taylor is a library wholesaler that can choose to carry titles from certain POD service providers' catalogs such as Lightening Source, but it is not guaranteed that they will carry your title.

Quality Books specialize in distributing to libraries. Certain guidelines must be met to be accepted for distribution. The submission guidelines and application is located at Quality-Books.com where you can download the distribution package.

You should be aware that applying for distribution through Quality Books does not guarantee distribution. They use a committee for the selection of tiles. Your book can not be previously exposed to the library market to be considered for distribution. Quality Books will not stock certain types of books, and you will need to read their guidelines. If accepted, you will mail a certain number of books per their request to be stocked on consignment. Publisher's compensation will begin after books are sold to the libraries.

As previously discussed, OverDrive.com is a supplier to libraries for digital books.

If you are unable to secure library distribution, you can do-it-yourself. The process will take research, time, and patience. The *American Library Directory* contains contact information for approaching libraries. You can start by locating the main branch in specific locations and contact the person in charge of acquisitions for your book's genre. You will need a library sales kit before you approach libraries.

The sales kit for libraries will use a different price sheet than the wholesale price sheet that was discussed at the beginning of this chapter. Some libraries will only purchase one book for their location while others will purchase a larger quantity. You will need to make a new price sheet for libraries. For one to six copies, you will charge the retail list price for the book with no quantity discount.

Library Discount Price Structure

Quantity	Discount	Price Per Unit
1 to 6 units	0%	$24.95
7 to 18 units	5%	$23.70
19 to 30 units	10%	$22.45
31 to 42 units	15%	$21.21
43 + units	20%	$19.96

You will provide the main branch with a complimentary copy of your book and sales kit. The main library branch will share your information with their fellow branches. The branch librarians will evaluate the sales material, and if they are interested in carrying your book, you will receive a purchase order within a few months.

Associations and groups that relate to your book's topic might be interested in using your book as a premium incentive for major contributors, current members, or new members. You can approach the associations and groups by mailing your sales kit with a personalized cover letter. You should follow-up with a phone call within a week to verify that your package was received and to ask if they have any questions. The follow-up call is a good technique for reminding the person about your package and the benefits that you can offer.

Non-profit organizations might be interested in using your book for a fundraising drive. The members of the organization will become the sales force. The organization can sell your book below the retail list price to be an incentive for buyers, and you give the organization a percentage from the total sales. Fund-raising is a win-win situation for both parties. Youth sports teams, cheerleaders, school clubs, senior citizen centers, and churches use fundraisers to raise money for their needs or the needs of the community.

You can approach local non-profit organizations in-person. You will need to take the price sheet out of your sales kit and replace it with a commission sheet that details the discount retail price, and a commission percentage that they will earn on each book sold.

Companies can purchase large quantities of books for various reasons such as employee enhancement, training, company branding, and to use for a promotional campaign. A self-help book could be used to motivate employees or give them a positive outlook. An instructional book can be used to train employees on new techniques and methods. A fiction book can be used for a promotional campaign as a giveaway.

Premium books are a lucrative market for a publishing company. A premium book is a pre-existing book that is customized for a company's exclusive use as a promotional vehicle to be sold or given away by the company. The company may decide to package the premium book with their products as an added value. You can resell your book multiple times to various companies.

The premium book concept is similar to an advertising specialty item, but the roles are reversed. You produce the promotional item (your book) that the company will pay to have their name, logo, ad message, and other customized extras on the product. This form of advertising can be kept by the receiver for many years due to the retainable value of the premium book.

The process of customizing a book for an individual company is only limited by the imagination. You can discuss the custom possibilities with the company. The book can be retitled to incorporate the name of the company. Their company logo can be added to the book's cover, and the history of the company can be added to the front matter of the book. Product coupons or incentives can be placed within the back matter of the book. The book's content can be slightly revised to include the company's name, service, or products.

You can brainstorm to identify companies who are a perfect fit to use your book as a premium. The company can be a service provider, a product manufacturer, or a chain of stores. A book about bartending recipes or a central character who is a bartender could be targeted at a liquor manufacturer, a liquor store chain, manufacturers who produce bartending type items, and bartending schools. Books about economics, financing, home buying, and investments could be a good fit for savings and loan companies, investment brokers, and insurance companies. There are numerous premium possibilities for a book.

Once you locate companies to target for premium books, you will mail your sales kit to the appropriate contact person within the company. The contact person will most likely be the head of marketing. You will need to personalize the cover letter to reflect the custom possibilities for their company, and how it will benefit them and their customers.

Premium books will require a new price sheet. The quantity discount for premium books average about sixty to eight percent and can start with a minimum quantity of 2,500 units. This structure is different from the wholesale price sheet due to the customized work involved for your publishing company with each order. Your cost per book will decrease with the high quantity print runs. The deep discount pays off with the large volume orders, and your profit can add up to substantial revenue for your company.

The example will use the same $24.95 book from the previous price sheets. The pricing of the book needs to be extremely attractive to buyers for high volume orders.

Premium Book Discount Price Structure

Quantity	Discount	Price Per Unit
2,500 to 5,499 units	60%	$9.98
5,500 to 8,499 units	65%	$8.73
8,500 to 12,499 units	70%	$7.48
12,500 to 18,499 units	75%	$6.24
18,500 + units	80%	$4.99

Manufacturers can be approached for product tie-ins that are a different promotional vehicle than premium books. Books used for product tie-ins are not a customized item, but the original book. A product tie-in is a promotional strategy for positioning two products together from different companies in the marketplace to increase awareness and sales. A product tie-in can breathe new life into an existing product by offering an added value that gives a competitive edge over the competition.

For example, you need to buy a tent for camping. There are several tents to pick from, and you have narrowed down your selection to two tents. The price difference between the two tents is a couple of dollars. One of the tents offer a free book inside the box about the scariest campfire stories, a ghost story, or outdoor survival techniques.

Even if the book does not interest you, will you buy the tent with the freebie? Most consumers will buy the tent with the freebie and giveaway the book as a gift if the topic doesn't personally interest them. Some consumers will be excited about the book and enjoy it for years to come. The tent with the added value achieved the sale over the competition and that is a major selling point.

There are many opportunities for books to be packaged with other products. Cookbooks can be packaged with baking sheets, pots and pans, blenders, and slow cookers. Books about finances, accounting, business plans, and marketing can be a tie-in for cash registers, credit card terminals, and bookkeeping software. Fiction books with a western genre can be packaged with country and western products. Romance books can be a good tie-in for products that women use like plush robes, house shoes, and lingerie. You should be creative to find the right fit for your book.

The same price sheet for premium books can be used for product tie-ins due to the high quantity volume.

A good resource is the *Thomas Register* for finding manufacturers to approach for special sales and located at ThomasNet.com. Another avenue is to make in-person contact with manufacturers by attending industry trade shows. You can do category searches for trade shows, conventions, and conferences at TheTradeShowCalendar.com and Conventions.net.

Chapter 7
Subsidiary Rights

Subsidiary rights are parts of a book or an entire book being licensed for a specific use by another party. An author owns the intellectual property rights to their literary work until they sign ownership over to another party. Intellectual property is a property right protected under federal and state law that includes copyrights, trademarks, and patents. The intellectual property holder can grant licensing rights by entering into a contract with another party. Licensing rights do not sign over ownership to the party, but allows the party to use the content for a specific purpose and for a certain amount of time.

You can acquire a subsidiary rights agent or do this on your own. If you take on this task yourself, you need to be knowledgeable about how to negotiate the terms of a contract or hire an attorney.

There are various rights that can be granted by authors who own the intellectual property rights to their book.

Serial rights are broken down into first serial and second serial. First serial is the right to publish specific excerpts from a book before the publication date. The second serial is the right to publish specific excerpts from a book after the publication date. Serial rights are usually granted to magazines and newspapers.

You should carefully choose the right media that can reach your target market to generate book sales. You should preselect material to pitch to the magazine or newspaper. Serial rights can be granted to more than one media outlet, but the excerpts should be different. First serial rights will be exclusive for the published material and require a waiting period before the book's release date.

Digital electronic rights are e-books and digital audio books. A publisher can grant specific territories for these rights or give worldwide distribution rights.

Reprint rights for mass market paperback can be targeted at a major publisher after your book is a success. When a book reaches a certain level of success, major publishers usually approach an independent publisher for reprint rights for mass market paperback.

Foreign sales and translation rights can be pursued through the *International Literary Market Place* directory book. If your book has the potential for foreign readers and the demand for it to be translated into various languages, you will want to pursue this avenue.

Motion picture rights and television rights are pursued through production companies and producers. An option can be purchased that reserves time for the buyer to pursue financing to go into production. If the financing is acquired, the pick up fee is paid to the author.

If your book has the potential to be turned into a movie, television miniseries, or documentary, you should consider pursuing this area. You can pitch your book for motion picture rights or television rights through online markets such as TVFilmRights.com where the entertainment industry scouts for acquiring these rights.

Merchandise rights are licensed to multiple manufacturers to produce brand name products. These products can be literally any item such as toys, bed comforters, and cell phone accessories that are sold with a real person, company, or fictional character's name, likeness, image, logo, slogan, and phrases on the item. Merchandise licensing can bring in more money than the other revenue avenues combine, think Harry Potter.

A book must be a commercial success before you can acquire merchandise deals. You can command better deals with a book that has been turned into a movie or television series. If your book has the potential for merchandise, you can put it in your promotional plan under a category for long-term goals.

Chapter 8
Manuscript Editing

———————————————————————

Manuscript editing is a series of edits that locate problematic areas within a manuscript. The four-step editing process is designed for complete focus on specific areas of the manuscript. A manuscript can remain problematic due to dealing with too many issues at once if there are not focal points.

An author can only edit to a point due to the closeness of the project. You wrote the content, and you know what the words are supposed to say, but sometimes, a person can add words that are not on the page or skim over misused words that have a different meaning. An author reads the manuscript the way it is intended, but in reality, your eyes and mind can deceive you. A fresh read of your manuscript by someone other than yourself can be very valuable with picking up problematic areas and providing valuable feedback.

There are many manuscript editing services available. Some companies offer an evaluation of your manuscript such as GreenleafLiteraryServices.com. The manuscript evaluation service is a great avenue to discover problematic writing areas that need work before the editing process begins. After the evaluation, you may decide to hire the professional service or handle the editing process on your own with proofreaders.

Personal resources can help you with the task of proofreading. You can make a list of friends and family who are avid book readers and excel in the specific areas of the editing process. Two to three people can proofread your manuscript. Keep in mind, people live busy lives and should be given a realistic deadline with plenty of time to read your manuscript.

The manuscript should be double-spaced for easy reading and to have room for editing remarks. You will need to instruct the proofreaders on the specific area of focus. The proofreader should underline the problematic area, and write a note next to the issue that explains what is wrong.

After you receive the edited manuscript back from the proofreader, you should ask for their honest overall feedback on the book. The key to receiving feedback is not to take it as a personal attack and get defensive, but you should listen to what the person has to say. You might discover that your manuscript needs additional work, if so, look at it as moving forward in a positive direction. You have spent too much time writing your manuscript to release it before it is ready.

The first stage in the four-step editing process is the content/story structure and writing style, which is the foundation of the manuscript. The edit involves the evaluation of the structure, movement, transitional flow, clarity, redundancies, content and chronological inconsistencies, correct historical or location facts, and correct usage of narrative tense.

An author's experience level and writing skills will determine the amount of rewriting or editing needed during this step. If you are a new writer to the world of fiction or creative nonfiction, you may need to take a creative writing class or study about the elements involved with creative writing. The same goes for a new nonfiction writer, who may need to learn the nonfiction techniques. Fiction and nonfiction are two completely different writing styles that involve key writing elements and skills. The exception is creative nonfiction writing, which can use the same techniques as fiction.

The author should evaluate the manuscript before sending it to a professional editing service or personal proofreaders. You will double check that the story clearly states the main conflict and what is at stake for the main character(s), has a climax, and a resolution. If your book is a how-to or instructional manual, you will double check the content for accuracy, easy comprehension, and a logical information structure.

For storylines, the transitions should flow from one setting to the next and from one character to another. For how-to or instructional content, the transitions should flow smoothly from one topic to the next, and you might consider using subtitles for the distinction.

The content should have clarity. You wrote the manuscript and have previous knowledge that the reader is lacking. You have to make sure a reader with no prior knowledge about the topic can understand the content with clarity.

Redundancies should be corrected where you repeat yourself by revealing the same information just in a different way.

Content and chronological inconsistencies should be double checked and can include: the contradiction of information, content presented out of order, inaccurate timeline within a story, and character inconsistencies.

Accurate facts are important with historical information, location settings, and anything else in your manuscript that could be deemed as inaccurate. You should do some fact-checking research to make sure your material is accurate.

Narrative tense should be correctly used and consistent throughout the manuscript.

You should delete the areas that do not move the story forward, or for an instructional manuscript, delete any areas that do not serve a specific learning or understanding purpose. Every word in your manuscript should be significant to the movement of the story or content. Fillers are areas with no real purpose and should be deleted. The main goal is to achieve a tight polished manuscript.

When the proofreaders are finished with editing the manuscript, you need to evaluate their comments. You should arrange to have a conversation with proofreaders to ask their overall opinion of the story and characters. Also, you should find out what they liked and didn't like about the story. For instructional manuscripts, you can ask their overall opinion about the content, if the information is explained well-enough for easy comprehension and in a logical learning order.

You should accept the good and the bad feedback as part of the development process. If you strongly disagree with a suggestion, you can leave it as is. If more than one person gives the same feedback, the issue needs to be taken into consideration for revision.

During this editing process, you should expect to make some changes after receiving feedback. Once you have completed the necessary manuscript changes, you will move on to the next editing stage.

The second stage in the four-step editing process is for writing and grammar fundamentals. This process involves spelling, grammar, sentence structure, punctuation, proper italics, and the correct usage of words. Every writer should own a copy of *A Writer's Reference* by Diana Hacker. This is a quick reference guide for proper writing and grammar as well as a valuable resource tool.

Before turning your manuscript over to a proofreader, you should read your manuscript out loud to help locate mistakes, and you can use Grammarly. com, which is a proofreading program that automatically proofreads in real time. The program reviews the content for grammar mistakes, provides an explanation of the error, and shows examples of how to fix the problem.

Next, you will be ready for the proofreaders. The proofreaders should understand the focus of this edit is for writing and grammar mistakes. You should always be open to other feedback.

If you receive feedback where there are a lot of mistakes, you might want to consider taking an English class at a community college, or you can get an English textbook to brush up on your writing skills. Once you have corrected the errors, you are ready to move on to the next stage.

The third stage in the four-step editing process is the overall effectiveness. This edit will not go to a professional editing service. The purpose of this edit is to receive overall feedback for promotional purposes.

You will make a list of four to six people, who are avid book readers or professionals in your topic field. At this point, you need new readers who have not previously been exposed to your manuscript to receive genuine feedback. You should ask the readers to write down their immediate thoughts about the book when they finish reading the manuscript. Also, you will ask the readers to mark any mistakes that might stand out to them.

For the positive feedback, you will ask permission to use the quote for promotional purposes and acquire the permission in writing.

You should fix any mistakes before sending the manuscript to a professional copy editor.

The final stage of the editing process is proofreading where you supply a polished manuscript to a professional copy editor or copy editing service. A copy editor is strictly looking for grammar mistakes. Most professional copy editing services charge by the word count of a manuscript.

You can check alternative resources to accomplish this task such as hiring an English teacher at a local school. People enjoy making extra money. The person should be familiar with editing your type of book such as business, creative writing, or academic. You should be able to locate a professional who is willing to do copy editing within your budget.

One or two mistakes are found in published books all the time, but excessive grammar mistakes reflect an amateur writer/publisher and a reason for reviewers to rip your book apart.

Chapter 9
Identify a Strong Book Title

Most authors have a working title while writing their manuscript, but you need to reevaluate the title once the manuscript is complete. A strong title gives a hint of what the book is about and captures the interest of a consumer by helping them make a buying decision.

The first thing a major publisher wants to change is an author's book title, because they know how important the title is for sales.

As the publisher, you must objectively consider a title change that best fits your book. Your book's title and cover are very important sales tools to attract potential buyers.

For example, the working title for the novel *Gone With the Wind* by Margaret Mitchell was *Pansy*, which reflected the name of the protagonist. Once the publisher got involved with the project, there was a title change and the main character's name changed. The protagonist's name became Scarlett O'Hara, and the title changed to *Gone With the Wind*. Could you imagine the elegant leading lady Scarlett O'Hara being named Pansy? In 1937, Mitchell won the Pulitzer Prize for *Gone With the Wind*. Do you think she would have won this coveted award with a title like *Pansy*? It is hard to say, but this is a prime example of a great title change.

To identify a good title for your book, you can brainstorm with other people or make a list of possible titles on your own. The list should be narrowed down, and you should seek input from other people about your best titles. Ask them, what they think the book is about when they hear the title, and would the title catch their attention enough to lure them into buying the book? You don't have to take other people's advice, but if more than one person does not like or understand the title, you should consider another title.

Chapter 10
Book Description, Author's Biography & Headshot

Before you begin the production process, you will need a compelling description of your book, a biography, and a headshot.

A book description is an opportunity to capture the attention of potential readers and acts as your most valuable sales pitch. A nonfiction description is a brief enticing summary of a book that contains the central idea and main points that support the central idea. A fiction description is a captivating summary of the storyline that contains the central plot and introduces the main characters.

The book description should be published on the back cover of the print format and audio book on compact disc. The description will be used during the book set up with service providers, which is used in their electronic catalogs for book wholesalers. Retail booksellers will publish the book description on the sales page for your book. You will use the description on all of your promotional materials.

The length of the book description can vary. The description should be written in the third person and present tense. You will tell the reader what your book is about in the most captivating way. If you have written a book with a storyline, do not reveal the ending of the story. You want to intrigue the reader into wanting more. If you have written a self-help book, instructional manual, or how-to guide, you will include what benefits the reader will obtain by reading the book and how it will satisfy their needs.

An author's biography (bio) is a summary about the author that can include published works, qualifications, educational degree, awards, skills, real life experience, achievements, and membership in key organizations. The summary of an author's biography is a way that people can learn about the author. The biography is used for setting up your book with service providers, press kit, interior of your book, official Website, and other promotional materials.

A biography is written in the third person and present tense. The only time you will use past tense in a biography is if you need to describe relevant experience or an event that happened in the past. The biography should be between fifty to a hundred words in length.

Your bio should be honest and to the point. Do not fill it with fluff. The introduction sentence should state your name. You need to focus on relevant information that relates to your book and what makes you qualified to write on this subject. The conclusion sentence will usually tell where the author resides. At the end of your bio, you should include your official Website address for readers that want to learn more about you and your book.

An author's photo (headshot) should be carefully planned before the photo shoot. You are creating a public image for yourself. How do you want to be perceived? Every aspect of your finished photo will create an image such as your hairstyle, choice of clothing, your expression, and tone of the photograph.

Some authors smile with or without showing teeth while others have a serious look on their faces. This comes down to the image that the author would like to portray to the public.

The focus of the photo is from the top of the author's head to below the chest area, not the background. You can implement a background setting for photos to use on your Website and social media sites, but you should consider a headshot for your main media photo and bio photo for your book.

A digital camera capable of producing 300dpi print quality should be used for the photo shoot. You can save money by not using a professional photographer, but the photo needs to look professional.

When setting up the photo shoot, you need to pay attention to the lighting, shadows, and background. The lighting should not be too harsh or too dark. You should sit or stand in the location where the photos will be taken. The person taking the photographs should look for shadows cast upon you that could distort your image. The background should be a solid color that is not the same color as your clothing or hair color. This keeps you from fading into the background.

The best photos are captured when the photographer continues to take photos as the person freely moves around in different positions with different expressions. When you stop to repose for each photo, it is harder to capture a natural look.

A large variety of photos should be taken in different positions and a variety of facial expressions. This way you have plenty of options to choose from later.

After you choose a headshot image, you can send the photo to a printing company such as ABCPictures.com, who specialize in headshots for the entertainment industry. You can order 8x10 headshots with your name on the photo for publicity purposes such as signing autographs for fans. You can have the photo retouched to get rid of unwanted blemishes and order electronic headshots.

You will need electronic headshots consisting of PDF and jpeg files for various reasons. The headshot image needs to be saved in full color as a high res 300dpi file, and a low res 98dpi file, and a high res 300dpi black and white file. The high res color files are used for traditional media, the book's production, and promotional materials. The low res files are used for the interior of an e-book, Internet, and online media. The high res black and white file is used for newspapers who print articles about you. There is no need for a low res black and white photo.

Chapter 11
The Structure of a Book

A book's structure consists of three elements called the front matter, the body of a book, and the back matter. The structure of a book and the key terms are important to understand the book's production process.

The interior of a print format has two key terms called the Verso and Recto that are used to describe the left and right pages. The Verso is the name of the pages located on the left side of a book's interior. The Recto is the name of the pages located on the right side of a book's interior. An easy way to remember the difference are the words "Recto" and "right" both start with the letter "R" for pages on the right. The Verso and Recto will be referenced throughout the book's interior sections. E-book formats do not reference Verso and Recto pages. The layout will not contain any blank pages unless you retain the print version format for the e-book.

The pages in a book that are located before chapter one begins are called the front matter. These pages can include the following: half title page, the title page, copyright page, author's biography, book quotes, other books by the same author, dedication, acknowledgements, table of contents, foreword, preface, introduction, and prologue. All of the above mentioned pages will not be included in every book, and it will be your choice to decide the book's content.

The half title page is the first page of a print format and is located on the Recto. The title of the book minus the subtitle is positioned a fourth of the way down the page. The same title font as the book's cover should be used on this page. Most authors use the half title page to sign autographs for readers. The half title page is not used in e-book formats. The Verso on the backside of the half title page is left blank.

The title page is the second page of the print format on the Recto side. The title page is the first page in an e-book after the front book cover image. The text on this page includes the full title including a subtitle, author's name, publisher's name or logo, and the city and/or state of where the publisher is located. The title and author's name should be in the same font as the cover. The title is positioned near the top of the page about a fourth of the way down. The author's name is positioned about three-fourths of the way down the page. The publisher's name or logo, and location are located at the bottom of the page. A special character symbol can separate the publisher's name from the city. The backside of the title page contains the copyright information.

The copyright page is located on the Verso and contains important legal and identification information. A copyright page is required for every published book.

Where the information starts will depend on the amount of text that you have for this page. If there is room, the top part of the page is usually blank, and the text starts about a third of the way down on the page.

A disclaimer is a legal statement that pertains to the contents of a book and is meant to protect the publisher and author from legal action arising from the content. For fiction, a disclaimer can state the characters and events in the book are fictional and the product of the author's imagination. For nonfiction, a disclaimer can state the publisher and the author assumes no responsibility of inaccuracies, errors, or omissions of the information contained in the book.

The copyright notice is a legal statement that states the book's copyright holder, warning for usage, and how to obtain permission for reprint. The copyright notice is usually in the form of a paragraph. The copyright line is stated as follows: "[Title of the book]. Copyright © [year and the name of the copyright holder]. All rights reserved." The warning of usage is next, which explains how no part of the book may be reprinted without the publisher's permission. Followed by an explanation of how someone can go about seeking reprint permission by contacting the publisher and the publisher's contact information is stated.

The copyright holder will depend on your desire for who holds the rights to your book such as you as an author or your company. There are pros and cons to both, which involves legal protection among other intellectual property right issues. In recent years, a few bestselling authors like Jackie Collins and Janet Evanovich have stopped using their personal name and started using their company's name as the copyright holder of their work. This is a legal matter where you would need to consult an attorney for further information. The copyright holder will need to be named on the U.S. Copyright application form.

Next on the copyright page, the book's identification information is provided. The International Standard Book Number (ISBN) is listed, followed by the Library of Congress Control Number (LCCN), and the Publishers Cataloging in Publication (P-CIP) information. If you are not distributing to libraries, you will eliminate the LCCN and P-CIP.

The next line states where the book was printed, for example, "Printed in the United States of America."

Next, the edition information is provided, for example, "First Edition: December 2011." When the content of a book is revised or updated, it becomes a second edition and will need a new ISBN assigned to the revised book.

At the bottom of the copyright page, credits can be given to the artistic and professional people involved with the book's production. Credits could be listed as shown in the example below.

Credits For Copyright Page

Book Layout by [first and last name]

Cover Design by [first and last name]

Edited by [first and last name]

Author Photograph by [first and last name]

A dedication is a thank you to a person or people who have made a difference in the author's life. The dedication starts on the Recto across from the copyright page. This page is optional.

Acknowledgements are sometimes included on the dedication page, in the preface, or part of the back matter. An acknowledgement is a thank you by the author to the important people who made a contribution to the book. The contributors can include people who offered creative ideas, conducted research, granted interviews, supplied information, and made editorial suggestions.

Book quotes and books by the same author appear on separate pages within the front matter. Both are considered valuable sales tools. The book quotes can help sell your current book to potential readers. The list of other books by the same author can help you obtain additional sales from readers who enjoyed your current book.

An author's biography (bio) is a summary of the author's accomplishments, qualifications, and expertise. The author's bio can be placed on the Recto or Verso. The author's photo can accompany the biography on the same page unless the photo is already used on the back cover of the print format. You have several choices with where to position the author's bio. With fiction books, the bio is usually positioned in the back matter, but can be located in the front matter. With nonfiction, the bio can be positioned in the front matter in order for the reader to know upfront the author's expertise for writing a nonfiction instructional manual or how-to book. With e-books, the bio can be located in the front or back matter.

The table of contents (TOC) is a quick reference outline that is set up in the order the contents appears in a book and can consist of a chapter number, chapter title, subtitles, and the page number that indicates where the information begins. A TOC can act as a point-of-purchase marketing tool where a potential consumer reads the TOC to make a final buying decision. This page can start on the Recto or Verso. A TOC is usually not used in the print format for fiction or creative nonfiction, but it is important to instructional manuals or how-to books. Every category and genre of e-books should have a TOC hyperlinked to each chapter.

A foreword is an informative piece about the book's topic. The foreword is usually written by a well-known person or a professional, who specializes in the topic field of the book. The foreword can start on the Recto or Verso page.

A preface is a description of why and how the book evolved from an idea into the end product and written by the author. Acknowledgements can be included in the preface. This page can start on the Recto or Verso.

An introduction is an explanation piece written by the author that describes who the book is for, the purpose of the book, and the author's goals for the reader. The introduction can start on the Recto or Verso. The introduction is important for self-help, how-to, and instruction manuals. An introduction can capture potential book buyers and is considered a marketing tool.

A prologue is an introductory scene that draws attention to a specific character and event that is presented before the first chapter of a fiction or creative nonfiction book. The prologue can give readers a glimpse of a future scene within the storyline similar to a preview. The prologue can start on the Recto or Verso.

The back matter is all of the pages that appear after the main story or content of a book. Back matter can include afterword, epilogue, appendix, bibliography, glossary, and index. All of the pages mentioned will not be included in every book.

An afterword is a final message from an author to a reader. The afterword can be placed on the Recto or Verso. The afterword can include a thank you to the reader and final thoughts.

An epilogue is a narrative or direct message from an author that brings closure to the characters by wrapping up loose ends beyond the storyline. An epilogue can be used to hint at a sequel. The epilogue is located on the Recto.

An appendix is supporting documents and additional material that is not supplied within the book's content. An appendix can start on the Recto or Verso.

A bibliography is cited works used to compile certain information within the book's content. This page can start on the Recto or Verso.

A glossary is the book's dictionary for important words found within the content. The words are arranged in alphabetical order along with the word's definition. A glossary can start on the Recto or Verso.

An index is a quick reference for locating important concepts, terms, topics, and names within a book's content. The words are arranged in alphabetical order preceded by a list of page numbers where the words appear in the content. The index can start on the Recto or Verso.

Chapter 12
The Production Process

The book production involves all of the aspects that go into constructing the book such as the cover, interior, and proofing the files for final approval. As a publisher, it is your job to get the book camera-ready for printing, digital files ready for downloading, and audio books ready for compact disc duplication. You can accomplish this by hiring professionals, using personal resources, or do-it-yourself. If you plan to hire a book production service, it is a good idea to get familiar with the production process and the terminology. This way you know what to look for during the proofing stages.

The production of a book can be a lengthy process, and the results can make you look like a professional or an amateur publisher. During the production, you must pay close attention to details. Once you give final approval, it is costly to fix any mistakes after that point.

An interior design is how the text and layout will appear on the pages of a book and consists of two main elements: typesetting and interior layout. A lot of decision-making takes place for the interior of a book. The book's interior must be easy-to-read and appealing to the eyes, which is accomplished through the typesetting and interior layout.

Most of the time, typesetting and interior layout are grouped together as one topic, but they are very distinctive layout elements.

The interior design of a book is done in a design program. For example, if you know a production designer familiar with Adobe InDesign, you can save money on your book's interior layout and typesetting for print and e-book formats.

Microsoft Word (MS Word) is an excellent word-processing program for manuscript writing and to use for the editing process. However, it is not a design program. Many of the vanity presses, who offer authors self-publishing services, will supply a MS Word template for a do-it-yourself layout. Most writers have MS Word, and it is an easy sales pitch for self-publishing services. Yes, it works, and many authors have published this way, but there are limited design options to this approach. Some e-book conversions can be accomplished with the manuscript in MS Word file, but certain items within the file will not convert.

When it is time to do the typesetting and interior layout, the MS Word file is imported into the design program. Before this takes place, you need to set paragraph indentations throughout your manuscript in the MS Word file. Do not use the tab key or space bar to achieve this goal or it will import with time-consuming problems that will need to be corrected. Turn on the "show paragraph marks and other hidden symbols" to make sure there is no extra spacing between words and sentences.

Whether you do-it-yourself or hire a professional, you need to understand typesetting and interior layout. Layout instructions should be provided to the professional designer. You will retain creative control and get what you want from the beginning without delay. Most design professionals appreciate when a customer knows what they want, and it makes their job easier.

Chapter 13
The Cover Design

━━━━━━━━━━━━━━━━━━━━━━━━━━━━━━━━━━━

A cover design for print formats and audio books on compact discs include the front cover, back cover, and spine of a book that is graphically balanced in design and color. The front cover image is used for e-books, digital audio books, and for promotional purposes. The spine and back cover are not used for digital book formats.

The front cover is your first chance to grab the attention of potential readers. A good front cover will effectively communicate what the book is about by providing a glimpse of the contents, grab the reader's attention, and help sell books by the cover.

You should study other book covers within the same genre to figure out a way to stand out from your competition. The entire cover layout can be viewed by opening a book to see how the design flows together. You should analysis the use of fonts, text, colors, and images.

The front cover includes the title and author's name. A sentence or tagline can be used as a quick description of the book. Sometimes, solid background color or variations of colors are used in the design. An illustration, photo, or image can be arranged in an appealing layout. The use of an author's photo on the front cover comes across as unprofessional and egotistical to some people. Unless you are famous or a recognizable public figure, your photo on the front cover is not going to help sell books or reveal what the book is about.

The back cover allows for variations of the design content. A short book description should appear on the back cover and a barcode that includes the book's ISBN.

Additional information can be added to the design. Many publishers include quotes that praise the book, a brief biography about the author, and a headshot on the back cover.

The spine includes the title and author's name. Many times, the publishing company's logo or name is placed on the bottom of the spine.

The cover for a print format will not be complete until the interior layout is finished. You need to know the number of pages in the finished layout to adjust the width of the spine.

The cover design should be submitted according to your POD service provider's guidelines, commercial book printer's requirements, or the manufacturer's requirements for compact disc duplication.

A graphic artist with production design experience can do the cover design. If you need an affordable design service, check out KillerCovers. com or 123PrintFinder.com. Print Finder provides typesetting, interior layout, and book cover design services. If you would like to pick your own image for the cover and supply it to the designer, check out Dreamstime. com and iStockPhoto.com. The copyright images on these Websites can be licensed at an affordable price. You should purchase the high resolution 300dpi image to meet quality printing standards.

The designer should be supplied with the text for your cover. If you have a high resolution image you would like to integrate into the design, you can supply the designer with the image, or the designer can locate an image to use for the design. Before approving the final cover design, you should carefully look over the file for any spelling or grammar mistakes.

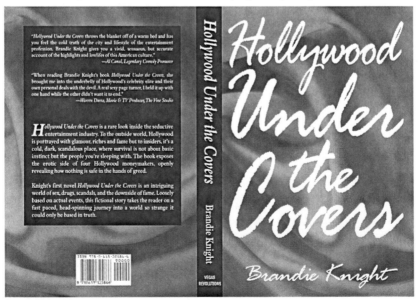

Book Cover Layout.

Chapter 14
Typesetting

Typesetting is how the type will appear on the interior pages such as the margins, font size, font, kerning, leading, widows, orphans, and justifications. All of these elements are very crucial to the readability of the book and to be acknowledged as a professional publisher and not an amateur.

There are four specific margins on a page for print formats: top, gutter (inside spine area), outside (opening of the book), and bottom. Right and left margins can not be set the same for every page due to the Verso and Recto being opposite setting. The margins are referred to as the gutter and outside. Verso pages have the gutter margin on the right, and Recto pages have the gutter margin on the left, which makes room for the book's binding area.

For example, a 6x9 print format can have the top, outside, and bottom margins set at .5 inches. The gutter margin should be .75 inches. You have to keep the text out of the gutter where the words are not lost in the binding area.

An e-book format can have the same size margins on all four sides. You may decide to design the print format first and make minor changes to the interior layout for the e-book. The margins from the print format can remain the same for the e-book, which gives it the look of a print book layout. Some e-book readers allow the consumer to view an e-book two pages at a time.

A font is a distinctive pattern for capital and lower case letters from A-Z, numbers, punctuation, and special characters. There are two main categories for fonts: serif typeface and sans-serif typeface. A serif typeface is a font designed with artistic details at the end of the letters, numbers, punctuation, and special characters. A sans-serif typeface is a uniformed font without the artistic details.

There are many serif and sans-serif fonts available but not all of them are suitable for typesetting. The serif fonts appear more often in novels such as New Baskerville, Garamond 3, and Palatino. The sans-serif font is popular in nonfiction, children's books, textbooks, and instruction manuals such as Gill Sans MT, Century Gothic, and Myriad. The same font should be used throughout the interior of the book for the primary body text, chapter titles, running heads, front matter, and back matter.

You will need to locate the interior font for your design needs. If you do not have the font on your computer, there are many Websites where you can acquire certain fonts for free. Fonts are copyrighted materials that may require you to buy or license the intellectual property. If you are using a production designer, you will include the font name in your instructions. There is a chance the designer already has the font of your choice or has a suitable font to meet your needs.

Font size is the size of the text that is measured by numbered point (pt) sizes. Several books use 11pt font for body text. The body text is the primary text located within the book's interior. Books targeted at older people with possible eyesight challenges from aging will be set in a larger font size and referred to as large print. Books for younger children learning to read will be set in a larger font size like 24pt to 30pt.

Serif Fonts

Garamond 10pt

New Baskerville Std   11pt

Palatino 20pt

San-serif Fonts

Gill Sans MT 10pt

Century Gothic 11pt

Myriad 20pt

Fonts and Point Sizes.

Chapter titles are usually in 20pt to 24pt font. Front matter and back matter are set one point less than the body text such as 10pt font.

Running heads are smaller than the body text and usually about 10pt font. A running head is a page header that is positioned above the body text that remains the same layout style throughout the book. Running heads should use the same font as the body text but appear different in style such as all caps, bold, or italics.

Running heads can slightly vary from book to book. A standard layout for the Verso pages of a book without chapter titles are in the following order: [page number] a few spaces to separate [author's name]. The Recto pages have the following order: [title of the book] a few spaces to separate [page number]. This layout has the page numbers on the outside of the page, not the inside where the spine is located.

In books with chapter titles, the running head for Verso pages are in the following order: [page number] a few spaces to separate [title of book]. The Recto pages have the following order: [chapter title] a few spaces to separate [page number].

Running heads do not appear on the front matter pages, chapter title pages, or any blank pages. The blank pages are counted for page numbering purposes. The back matter of a fiction and creative nonfiction book usually will not contain running heads. The back matter of a nonfiction book will have running heads.

Running Heads For a Book Without Chapter Titles

Verso Page	Recto Page
12 *BRANDIE KNIGHT*	*HOLLYWOOD UNDER THE COVERS* 13

Running Heads For a Book With Chapter Titles

Verso Page	Recto Page
28 *SELF-PUBLISH LIKE A PRO*	*THE MARKETING MIX* 29

A chapter title page is an indication of a break in the story or a change of topic within the theme of a book. Chapter title pages can be formatted in one of three ways, but it must be consistent throughout the book.

Chapter title pages that "fall into place" start on the next Verso or Recto page following the end of a previous chapter that leaves no blank pages within the body of the book.

"Recto chapter title pages" always begin on the Recto and may or may not leave a blank page on the Verso, which is located on the opposite side of the chapter title page.

"Stacking chapter title pages" is when the previous chapter ends and a new chapter will begin a few lines beneath it on the same page.

A chapter title can begin about one-fourth to one-third of the way down from the top of the page. The chapter title should include the chapter number and name of the chapter, if any.

Chapter title pages have a uniformed style and layout that involves the font size of the chapter titles, possible drop caps on the first word of the first paragraph, indention or no indention for the first paragraph, and possibly the use of illustrations, which is added during the interior layout.

Fall Into Place

Verso Page	Recto Page
	Body of Content
Chapter 14	Body of Content
Body of Content	Body of Content
Body of Content	Body of Content
Body of Content	Body of Content
Body of Content	Body of Content
Body of Content	Body of Content
Body of Content	Body of Content

Chapter Title Pages.

Recto Chapters

Verso Page	Recto Page
Last chapter ended on previous page	Chapter 14
	Body of Content
Blank Page	Body of Content
	Body of Content
	Body of Content
	Body of Content
	Body of Content

Stacking Chapters

Verso Page	Recto Page
Body of Content	Body of Content
Body of Content	Body of Content
Body of Content	Body of Content
Body of Content	Body of Content
	Body of Content
Chapter 14	Body of Content
Body of Content	Body of Content
Body of Content	Body of Content

Chapter Title Pages.

Leading, kerning, and tracking allow a designer to adjust spacing between baselines, letters, and punctuations for better readability and to achieve a structured balance of blank spaces.

Leading (pronounced led-ing) is the vertical spacing between baselines also referred to as "line spacing" in word-processing programs. A baseline is the imaginary line the letters sit upon within the text. Some letters descend below the baseline such as g, y, and p. In a graphic design program, leading is measured in points and should be 2 to 3 points greater than the font size. For example, this book has a layout of 11/14, which means the font size is 11pt, and the leading is 14pt.

Kerning is the individual letter spacing between two letters of a word that appear too loose with gaps or too tight with overlapping. Positive kerning will loosen the letters, and negative kerning will tighten the letters. There are certain letter combinations when placed next to each other in a word create an unbalanced look to the layout, and kerning will fix the problem.

Tracking is the letter spacing between letters within words that create uniform spacing for groups of words in a headline, sentence, paragraph, and blocked text.

Widows and orphans are a sign of an unprofessional typesetting job. A widow is the last line of a paragraph that moves on to the top of the next page. The first line of a paragraph that is left behind at the bottom of a page is an orphan. There is an old saying to remember the difference between the two terms, "A widow must go on, and an orphan is left behind." An "orphan word" is the last word of a paragraph that ends up on the final paragraph line alone.

Widows and orphans can be eliminated by a minor rewrite to the paragraph, a slight adjustment to the leading, or by making a page slightly shorter or longer. The objective to eliminating widows and orphans is to do it without drawing attention to the change. You want to keep the look of a uniformed layout throughout the book. You should let the designer know if you would like to fix the widows and orphans by doing a slight rewrite to the paragraphs.

Text justification is an alignment of text between the margin settings. There are two types of alignments to pick from: left align and full justify. A left alignment aligns the text flush against the left margin setting to achieve a clean, uniformed appearance on the left side of the page. The text on the right margin will not be uniformed. Full justify aligns the text to be flush against the left and right margin settings to achieve a clean uniformed appearance on the left and right sides of the page. The text justification should be consistent throughout the layout of a book.

Widow, Orphan & Orphan Word

Verso Page

This is an example of a paragraph that contains an orphan word.

The paragraph above shows "word" on the the last line by its self.

This is an example of a paragraph that contains a widow. The last line of this paragraph is on the

Recto Page

next page alone.

The paragraph above shows how a single line should not be separated from the paragraph.

If the last paragraph on the previous page had left behind the first line, it would be an example of an orphan.

Widows and Orphans.

With full justify, each line within a paragraph becomes the same length. Words can stretch to add extra spacing. When using full justify, the last line in a paragraph should be set for a left alignment, otherwise, the last line stretches to reach both margins.

For the rest of the paragraph, full justify can create a problem when a word at the end of the line will not fit, and it is moved to the beginning of the next line. The remaining words on the original line are stretched to compensate for the extra room, which creates extra word spacing. This issue can be eliminated by a minor rewrite or by forced hyphenation. Forced hyphenation is a manual syllable breaking point of a word that is divided with a hyphen. In a graphic program, there is a hyphenate setting that will allow the forced hyphenation.

The first line of a paragraph should be indented about a quarter inch (0.25). The first line of a paragraph following the chapter title is customarily given no indention, but this is a preference, not a rule. A typesetter will set paragraph style settings and should never use the tab key for indention purposes.

Inner blocking is a paragraph formatted by setting new left and right margins within the body text to distinguish the paragraph from the primary text. A 0.50 inch margin is set on the left and right for the inner blocking paragraphs.

Text Justification

This is an example of a paragraph with a left align. The text is even on the left side of the paragraph, but uneven on the right side.

This is an example of a paragraph with full justify and force hyphenation. The paragraph is uniformed on the left and right side.

Inner Blocking

This is an example of inner blocking a paragraph. The text stands out from the rest.

Text Justification and Inner Blocking.

With creative writing, the inner blocking is used when a character is listening to voice mail, news broadcasts, a television program, reading a letter, an article, an e-mail, or a text message that is vital information for the reader. Flashbacks can use inner blocking or italics.

For nonfiction, inner blocking is used to set off quotations of five or more lines. The inner blocking can be used for presenting examples that are in text form.

Chapter 15
Interior Layout

Interior layout is the arrangement of illustrations, graphics, or photographs in an eye-pleasing balanced environment within a book's interior. These items must be 300dpi (dots per inch) to be used for quality printing purposes. E-books usually require an item to be 98dpi for quicker downloading and smaller file sizes.

Once these items are integrated into the interior layout, a caption, and a permission statement should be added to the design. A caption is a brief description of an illustration or photograph used in an interior layout. A permission statement is a legal acknowledgement of a copyright holder. On the side of an image, a permission statement can be positioned vertically and read, "Courtesy of [copyright holder's name]" in 8pt or 9pt font. The permission statement can appear on the copyright page in the front matter or by the placement of the image within the interior.

If you hire a graphic artist to design specific artwork, this is considered "work for hire" where you are contracting out the work to a professional. You should have a written agreement with the individual or company that states the item to be designed, the agreed upon fee, and it should state that your company will own the copyright. If a contract agreement is not in place, the artist can try to claim ownership of the copyright.

If you contract a photographer for a photo shoot, you should have a "work for hire" written agreement. If you take the photograph, you own the copyright. If you use a pre-existing photograph or illustration you must have reprint permission, and you might have to pay a licensing fee to use the image.

If you use a color photograph with a black and white interior, your print format will be considered a color interior, and you will be charged for color printing. All items must be turned into a halftone for the print format to be considered a black and white interior. For an e-book, items can be in color, black and white, or a mixture of both.

Any illustrations or graphic items that are used as an example of a technique being explained within the text should be positioned after the explanation. If the example appears before the explanation, it will not make sense to the reader.

Chapter title pages can have a stylish layout that involves the use of illustrations, photographs, or graphic images.

The length of the process to prepare, scan, and position items for the interior layout can vary, and it depends on the number of images that will be used within the book's interior.

Once the initial layout is finished, the designer will supply you with a PDF file to proof. You can type your changes in an e-mail by supplying the page number, paragraph number, line number, and instructions for the change. Any text that you want inserted into the layout should be placed within quotation marks. You will keep a copy of your requested changes and check the corrections when the designer supplies you with the revision file to proof.

You will need to pay close attention and take your time proofing the typesetting and interior layout. When you give final approval, the file will be prepared for the printer. You will have two extra expenses to fix the problems if mistakes are found after the file submission. You will be faced with paying the designer to fix the issues, and you have to pay the service provider another set up fee.

There are two files that need to be submitted to the service provider: the book cover file and the interior file.

Once you receive a physical book proof from your service provider, you will need to give another final approval. You should check the book for print quality of the cover and the layout of the interior pages. If there is a problem, it will most likely stem from the camera-ready files that you submitted to the service provider.

After you give final approval on the POD, your service provider will make your book available in their digital catalog for distributors and for you to place book orders.

Chapter 16
E-book Design,
Formatting & Conversion

Formatting an e-book on various reading devices can be a challenging task. If you lack personal resources that are knowledgeable about this process, there are professional companies who specialize in e-book design, formatting, and conversions. Joshua Tallent is one of the leading experts in the e-book industry. His company eBookArchitects.com provides services such as e-book conversions to the various formats, designing, and formatting of an e-book and enhanced e-book at affordable prices.

Numerous e-books contain poor design compatibility and readability. The main design problem is when the e-book is formatted to be viewed on a large screen like a tablet or computer, but the e-book is difficult to read on small, portable devices. The industry has developed the QED seal of approval to solve this issue. QED stands for quality, excellence, and design. The presence of a QED seal on the front cover of an e-book assures the distributor and consumer that the book will function properly at the highest quality. The QED Website located at QED.DigitalBookWorld.com will inspect your e-book, and either, award a QED seal of approval or deny your request due to design issues. If you use eBookArchitects.com, they produce quality e-books and acquire the QED seal of approval for you as part of their service.

If you would like to do the file conversion yourself to publish on Amazon, Kindle Direct Publishing (KDP) offers an avenue for Kindle e-book conversion from an Adobe InDesign file or Microsoft Word file. Before you decide to take on this task, you should read the Amazon's KDP community forum for issues that arise from the file conversion process and read KDP guidelines.

Before you begin the e-book process, you will need to consult the most current guidelines and content restrictions from your e-book service providers. For example, as of this publication date, Barnes & Noble's

Publt! will not allow hyperlinks, book review requests, advertisements, promotional materials, or contact information for the author or publisher within the e-book design. However, Amazon's Kindle Direct Publishing will permit these items. If the content restrictions are not followed, your self-publishing account will be terminated.

The book cover and interior design files of your print format can be used to format your e-book. If you bypassed creating a print version of your book, you should ask the e-book designer what type of file to submit and if the initial layout should be finished ahead of time.

The front book cover will be used for the e-book, but the spine and back cover are eliminated from the design. Certain e-book submissions require the front cover to be the first page of the e-book while others require separate files or both.

If you are using the print format file to convert to an e-book format, the half title page should be eliminated, and the designer should replace it with the front cover image. This concept will keep the layout intact where the Verso and Recto pages remain on the correct sides.

The front book cover, author's photo, and other images such as illustrations, photographs, and graphics can be in full color. A low dpi resolution is required for an e-book such as a 98dpi. Your service provider's e-book guidelines will provide the submission requirements.

Active hyperlinks should be present in the e-book design for the e-book distributors that allow this function. There are internal and external hyperlinks. The internal hyperlink is a way of linking information inside the e-book such as the table of contents (TOC), index, and glossary. The TOC will need to have active hyperlinks to take the reader directly to the chapter title pages. If your book does not have a TOC in the print format, one can be designed with chapter numbers that are active hyperlinks. You can be creative with how you use internal hyperlinks by linking specific information together.

The external hyperlink is a way of linking information from within the e-book to outside sources such as Websites, e-mail addresses, and sales pages for your other books. For example, you can include a "review this book" external hyperlink on the last page of your e-book. The hyperlink will take the reader to your book's sales page where the book review section is located. Positive reviews help increase book sales.

You will want to include your official Website address with an active hyperlink on the copyright page or the author's bio page.

Depending on your service provider's guidelines, you may need a new ISBN for the e-book format. You will go to MyIdentifiers.com, log in to your publisher's account, and assign an ISBN to the specific book format. The ISBN will need to appear on the copyright page of the e-book.

An enhanced e-book is only limited by your creativity. There is a current debate about what type of supplemental material should be included in an enhanced e-book. Some critics believe the additional content should not include self-promoting materials, but it should focus on aspects that enhance the story or topic. The enhanced materials will be left up to you since you retain full creative control over your book. The following information is offered as possible suggestions.

Videos, audio, images, or hyperlinks can appear throughout the book's content if the material directly relates to the story or topic. Otherwise, you may want to supply the additional material where it is not integrated into the content.

A book with a storyline can have a music soundtrack in the form of audio or music videos. This is the same concept as a movie soundtrack.

A story based on a true event can include behind-the-scenes interviews with people that were there, or experts who are knowledgeable about the event such as researchers. Archived videos and photos can be used. Archival materials can include news footage, media articles, historical artifacts, and factual information.

A fictional story can include an interactive character tree of how the characters are connected or a character's family tree. Fictional history, myths, and facts can be included about the characters, culture, and setting.

A how-to book or instructional manual can integrate videos that illustrate difficult tasks. Instructional videos can replace illustrations and example images.

Author interviews can be included, and an audio book can be offered as part of the enhanced e-book package.

Remember if you do not self-create the enhanced materials, you will need to acquire permission from the copyright holder to use the material.

Apple has a free app called iBooks Author where you can design a Multi-Touch e-book for iPad. You can create your enhanced e-book by using a pre-set template and the simple drag and drop feature for text, videos, galleries, and more. Your interactive Multi-Touch book can be distributed in Apple's iBookstore and iTunes. The iBooks Author app is available for free in the Mac App Store. For more information about iBooks Author go to Apple.com/iBooks-Author.

After the design is complete, the e-book will need to be converted into various e-book format files.

During the e-book conversion approval process, you will need to proof the layout before giving final approval. Your e-book designer will supply you with links to download the various e-reader programs to view each e-book format. You should check that the hyperlinks are properly working. With an enhanced e-book, check the added materials to make sure everything is properly functioning. If the author's name is appearing unknown within the e-book reader library, this is a result from the author's name not being typed into the properties area of the original file.

You should note any changes that need to be made to the files and submit the changes for revisions, if any. Once the files are returned, you will proof the revisions and double check the rest of the file.

Once you give final approval on the e-book conversion files, you will be ready to set up your e-book with your service providers.

Chapter 17
Audio Book Production

The audio book production can be accomplished in one of three ways: hire a professional audio company, do-it-yourself, or utilize personal resources. Audiobook Creation Exchange (ACX) offers professional audio book production as well as an option to distribute through their distribution partners. For more information, ACX is located at ACX.com. Audacity offers free audio recording software to do-it-yourself at Audacity. SourceForge.net. If you know a band or someone that has a home recording studio, you can take advantage of their equipment and expertise to accomplish this time-consuming task.

There are several decisions to make when producing an audio book. The first is to decide if you will produce an unabridged or abridged audio book. An unabridged version is a word-for-word narration of the full content within a book, which many consumers prefer. An abridged audio book is a shorter edited version of a book's content. The purpose of an abridged version is some consumers prefer a shorter version of the content due to the length of an audio book being excessive.

An audio book is produced by recording a narrator(s) reading the content of a book. Books without a storyline can be narrated by one person: the author or someone with a pleasant voice. You must take into consideration that the consumer will be listening to this voice for hours, and the narrator should not have an irritating tone of voice. Books with a storyline can be narrated by the author, a couple of people, or a group of people cast to read for different characters.

A fully dramatized audio book can consist of a cast of narrators, sound effects, and music. The sound effects and music are optional.

Fully dramatizing an audio book is comparable to an actor doing voiceover for animated movies. Narrators should use inflection in their voices to bring the characters to life. For example, when the story calls for specific feelings to be revealed to the listener, the narrator should play the part by sounding excited, sad, or shy. A narrator should remain in character throughout the reading of the story.

If you decide to take on the challenge of an audio drama with a group of local narrators, you can cast people to read for various characters. Voiceover talent can be recruited by contacting your local theater actors, radio personalities, or friends. You will need to direct your narrators' performances to deliver what you have envisioned for your audio book.

You can organize a call sheet for each narrator. You will go through your book and write down the characters from each chapter, and the page numbers that each character appears within the story. The book should be recorded by chapters and each file saved as the specific chapter number, but the chapters can be recorded out-of-order. For example, if a character appears in chapters six and nine, you can record both of those chapters in a day with that narrator only showing up for one day of recording. Supply each narrator with the day and times that he/she will be needed to record the character's part. Supply each narrator with a copy of your book and the page numbers where the character appears. This allows the narrator to read over the part and get familiar with the character before showing up for the recording session.

Music can be present as an intro in the beginning of the audio book and at the end. You may decide to include music throughout the story as a soundtrack or sound effects to enhance the audio drama. You can compare this to a movie where music or sounds are used to set the tone of a scene or increase the intensity of a vital moment within the story. Remember music and sound effects are copyrighted materials, and you must acquire permission to use the materials unless it is public domain.

If you are doing the audio recording yourself, it is a good idea to use an external hard drive to backup the files at the end of each recording session. Depending on the length of your book, you could end up with many hours of audio files, and you do not want to risk losing your hard work.

Before you begin recording, you will need a computer, audio recording software, unidirectional microphone, and a soundproof room. Unidirectional microphone records sound from the direction the microphone is pointed and cuts down on unwanted noises.

The recording room should not echo and be free of background noises. To soundproof a room, you will need to hang blankets on the walls and over the windows. You will roll up a towel to place under the door, and you need to turn off items that make noise such as a heater, air conditioner, fans, and electronic equipment.

A book stand will save your arms from getting tired and help to keep your head at the same level during the recording session. An adjustable music stand works well to hold your book. Place the stand behind the unidirectional microphone so it does not pick up the noise from turning the book's pages.

You should sit in a comfortable, stable chair that does not rock back and forth. The book stand should be within arms reach behind the microphone and within an area where the readability of the words is not strenuous on your eyes.

At the beginning of each recording session, you will need to do a sound check. Record a vocal test by reading a few sentences from your book. The recording should be played back to ensure the equipment is properly working, and the sound level is adequate.

If you are using the Audacity software, you will need to hook up the microphone first and open the program second. Otherwise, the software will not recognize the microphone. You can use the built-in microphone on your computer, or an external unidirectional microphone, which will result in a professional quality recording.

Depending on the length of your book, there will need to be multiple recording sessions. You need to be well-rested and in a good mood when you record your audio book. When you feel tired and worn out, it is best to stop recording for the day, because your fatigue will reflect in the sound of your voice.

During the recording process, if you record one chapter at a time and save it to a file named after the chapter number, it will give your voice time to rest, and it will be easier to edit later. You should keep each chapter in a separate audio file for the different tracks on the finished product.

If you make a mistake while reading the book, you should keep recording by pausing for a couple of seconds and reading the words again. This approach allows you to edit out the mistakes later and saves you time during the recording session. Otherwise, you have to stop, edit out the mistake, start recording again, and get repositioned to record.

You will need to record the spoken credits to insert at the beginning and end of the audio book. The opening credits should include the book's title, "written by [author's name]" and "narrated by [narrator's name]."

The closing credits should include "this has been [book's title], written by [author's name] narrated by [narrator's name], copyright [year and name of copyright holder], production copyright [year of the recording] by [company's name]." In the closing credits, you should include any permission granted by copyright holders.

Once you finish editing the audio book, you will export the audio to MP3 or WAV file format. You should check with your service provider's guidelines for the required file format.

When you export a file, you will be prompted to fill in the ID3 tags, which help consumers identify the file on their media player.

A one to five minute sample of your audio book should be produced as a preview for consumers. You can use this as a promotional tool on various Websites to promote your audio book.

A new ISBN will be required for each audio book format. You will go to MyIdentifiers.com, log in to your publisher's account, and assign an ISBN to the specific book format.

For a digital audio book, you will need the finished audio file, know the finished length of the audio recording, and your book's front cover image at a low resolution. You will need to check your service provider's guidelines for submission details.

For an audio book on compact disc, you can use a print-on-demand service that prints and distributes audio books or a compact disc manufacturer with duplication services such as DiscMakers.com. Besides submitting the audio file, you will need to supply camera-ready artwork for the packaging that matches your book's cover but with a new ISBN and barcode. Artwork to be printed on the actual compact disc will need to be supplied. You will need to check the service provider's guidelines for submission details.

Chapter 18
Advance Preparations

There are important preparations that need to be accomplished several months prior to the book's publication date. Before the preparations can begin, your publishing company should be established as a legal entity, the title of the book identified, the book description written, and service secured through service providers. You will need the front cover of your book designed for various registrations and services that will be used for sales and promotional purposes.

The finished book size and the amount of pages need to be established in order to set the book's price and to supply the information for setting up the title, trade listings, and registrations. The number of pages will not be confirmed until after the interior layout is complete, but you need a close estimate to move forward.

The type of book, trim size, paper weight, paper color, interior black and white or color, and page count will determine your cost per print format. You can refer to the print-on-demand guidelines for the book spec choices. Does your book have black and white interior or color interior? What type of book do you want to publish: small paperback or large paperback? Trim size is also known as a finished book size, and there is a wide range of sizes. Depending on your POD service provider, you should be able to choose your own paper weight, which is usually around 50lb to 55lb. The choice of paper color is usually white or crème. Some people believe white is harder on the eyes and prefer crème.

The page count is determined by different production variables such as the finished book size, font, the font size, leading, the text alignment, how chapter title pages are set up, and editing widows and orphans. Once the estimated page count from the manuscript is determined, pages will need to be added for the front matter, back matter, and space requirements for any illustrations, photos, or artwork.

By evaluating the example below, you will see how each double-spaced manuscript page becomes 1.24 interior layout pages. You can divide 442 pages by 1.24 to reach the figure of 356 pages. Add the 8 pages for the front and back matter to end up with the 364 pages. You will add extra pages for illustrations, photos, and graphics to get an estimate of your final page count.

The following is an example of a double-spaced manuscript with 442 pages and 92,172 word count.

Book Specs & Estimated Page Count

Trim size: 6x9

Font: ITC New Baskerville STD

Font size: 11pt

Leading: 14pt

Text Alignment: Full justify

Front matter: 6 pages front and back

Back matter: 2 pages front and back

Illustrations/photos/artwork: 0

Interior layout pages: 356 pages

Total front and back page count: 364 pages

*Note: Front and back pages are counted including blank pages. Do not count the author's headshot as an extra page, because the bio page will be counted as part of the front or back matter pages.

The retail list price and wholesale price can be established once your cost per unit is determined. Your POD service provider's manual should contain a price chart for printing cost. You may choose to increase the retail list price by two to three dollars for padding in case the estimated page count runs over in the final interior design, and then, proceed with the book price formula discussed in chapter four.

If your book contains content protected under the Copyright Act, you will need to get reprint permission from the copyright holder to use the material. You will send a cover letter and a release form to the copyright holder to acquire written permission for reprint.

The publication date is the date a book is made available to the public and often referred to as a release date. Have you ever wondered why major publishers have a long lead-time before a book is published? There are several advance preparations to take into consideration when setting a publication date such as the production time, pre-promotion, and presales. Prepublication lead-times are important for Publishers Cataloging in Publication, book reviews, trade listings, library distributors, and subsidiary rights.

One of the advantages of self-publishing is you are the driving force behind this venture. You have the option to rush your book into the marketplace or take full advantage of key publicity and extra revenue streams by setting an extended publication date.

You will greatly benefit by being patient with publishing your book. Once a book passes the publication date, you can no longer take advantage of the prepublication opportunities.

An extended publication date gives you time to take advantage of the prepublication period to create hype for the release date. Before and after you have the printed books in hand, you can secure reviews, book quotes, and book listings to acquire presales. You can secure first serial rights. The prepublication period is an exciting time for you as an author and publisher.

Once you figure out a time frame, you should add two to three months to set your publication date. Things do go wrong and fall behind schedule. The extra months will ensure a well-prepared release date.

There are certain times of the year to be cautious about setting your publication date. A publication date should not be set during financially straining months such as after Christmas, or during the time parents are purchasing back-to-school supplies and clothes for their children. You may decide to release your book when people receive federal refund checks or around a certain holiday that can tie into your book's topic.

You might consider staying away from a publication date toward the end of the year. Many awards and services have guidelines that they only include books with the current year's copyright and publication date. Some companies will make an exception for books released in November or December and some will not.

When setting your publication date, you should give yourself enough time to accomplish your promotional plans that include properly timed materials and prepublication activities.

As previously discussed, if you are planning to engage in the library distribution and sales, you will need to apply for the LCCN and P-CIP. The LCCN can be acquired by going to Loc.Gov/Publish/PCN and applying for the free Pre-assigned Control Number (PCN). The process usually takes about one to two weeks to receive the LCCN. After you have the LCCN, you will need to hire a cataloging agent such as FiveRainbows.com or Quality-Books.com to receive a P-CIP block. The P-CIP block should be placed on the copyright page of your book and will contain the LCCN.

You can apply for library distribution through a service provider such as Quality-Books.com at least four months in advance of your publication date. If you use Lightning Source as a service provider, Baker & Taylor could pick up your book for library distribution through LSI's book catalog. If you are turned down for library distribution, you will need to contact libraries directly as soon as your book formats and promotional materials are in your hands.

Depending on the requirements of your service provider, you will assign an ISBN to each book format. You will login to your publisher's account at MyIdentifiers.com and click on the "Manage ISBN" tab. After you submit the book details, you will be registered for *Books in Print.*

You need to register your title about four months in advance with the trade directories and publications. The submission guidelines for upcoming titles and book reviews should be acquired in advance for the *Library Journal* by going to LibraryJournal.com, *Independent Publisher* at Independent-Publisher.com, and *Publishers Weekly* at PublishersWeekly.com.

Before your publication date, you can register your title with the U.S. Copyright Office. The online registration is located at Copyright.Gov. You can register, pay online, and print a shipping label to mail the print format to U.S. Copyright Office to complete the registration.

As previously discussed, you can solicit first serial rights at least seven months before your publication date. There will be a release clause in the contract that states a specific period of time must pass from the time your article is published in the periodical until the publication date. You need time to plan for this release clause.

A sales package should be put together to solicit serial rights with a cover letter, book cover image, and a copy of the table of contents. The cover letter should include the book's description and the author's biography. After studying the magazine or newspaper, you will preselect excerpt material to suggest for publication and include it in the sales package. If the media are interested, they will request a finished book for review. As part of the agreement, you should require the media to include your copyright notice and the information where your book can be purchased as part of the published article.

The trade association representing independent publishers is Independent Book Publishers Association at PMA-Online.com If you become a member of this association, you will have networking opportunities, various production discounts, valuable resources, and educational opportunities.

Chapter 19
Pre-promotion Equals Presales

Promotion is the strategic efforts used to reach and inform consumers about a product for the sole purpose of generating sales. Promotional strategies require brainstorming and research to create an effective promotional plan. Promotional concepts are the elements to develop a strong foundation for your book's promotion that can result in substantial revenue for your publishing company.

The promotion for your book should begin three to four months before your publication date. The purpose is to build hype and anticipation for your book's release which will secure presales.

During the "title set up" with service providers, you will be asked the publication date, which is the date your book will be released to the public. Most service providers will launch a sales page for your book in advance to acquire presales. Your job is to direct customers to the book's sales page through your promotional efforts.

Shopping and selling online is becoming the preferred method of economic transactions due to the convenience and instant gratification that it offers. The Internet is vital to a book's promotion. Effective Internet marketing is time-consuming, but it can be accomplished with low-cost marketing techniques.

Social media are Web-based platforms used for global interaction with user-generated content. Some of the top social media sites are Facebook and Twitter. These sites are free to the user and create an opportunity to connect with an enormous amount of people around the world.

These sites are free promotional vehicles that create exposure, build branding for the author with Internet presence, and generate book sales. The sites provide a way to keep in touch with your readers by informing them of your upcoming events and hyping up the release of a new book to create anticipation and prepublication sales.

Once you create an account on a social media site, you can start building a network of followers from around the globe. You should target potential readers, who enjoy bestselling authors of the same genre as your book, by going to the author's fan page and doing searches for people who like the authors. For example on Facebook, you can go to the author's fan page and send friend invites to the person's fans. The friend invite should include a short note that reads, "Hi, I am a big fan of [author's name] too. You might be interested in my new book, [name of book]. If not, I'm sorry to bother you." Be careful about sending out too many friend requests in one day. Facebook has a no spam policy where you will be warned about your behavior, and if it continues, your account will be closed. Many people will accept your friend request and purchase your book if it interests them.

An official Website and a blog are essential promotional vehicles. You will give out your Website address to the public, media, and on all promotional materials to lure as many visitors to your site as possible.

The first step is to secure domain names for the author's name, the title of your book, and publishing company name. You can pay to host one of the three sites, the author's Website, through your hosting provider such as GoDaddy.com. You can forward the book's title and publishing company domains to the author's site. The Internet browser will redirect the two Web addresses to the author's Website.

The domain forwarding is important for promotional reasons. If your name is difficult to spell, you should give out the book's title Web address over the air when conducting a radio or podcast interview. For print interviews, Internet interviews, and promotional materials, you can supply your author's Web address, because the Website address will be in print. Another important aspect to using your author's Web address is to brand yourself in the market as an author. You want people to know and remember your name to build a loyal fan base of readers.

There are a minimum of three main e-mail addresses to set up on the author's Website. Your publishing company e-mail, publicity inquires e-mail, and author's personal e-mail.

The next step is to have the author's official Website designed. Several major corporations use WordPress, which is a blogging platform, as their main Website. You can get the look and feel of a real Website by using a third-party WordPress template. You do not need prior Web design experience, because WordPress is simple to design and maintain.

You can integrate your official Website and blog into one promotional tool. First, you should know the function of a blog and WordPress to understand this concept design.

A blog is a personal journal or themed articles published on a Web Content Management System (WCMS). The WCMS is Web authoring software that is easy to design and update without Web design experience.

A new media outlet has emerged with the creation of blogs where the owner of the blog can write, publish, and attract loyal subscribers from around the world. A blog is mostly written articles but can feature videos that would be of interest or helpful to your readers. An author's blog is a valuable promotional vehicle for promoting a book.

Blogging platforms such as WordPress have Search Engine Optimization (SEO) as part of the design, and the capability to add SEO plug-ins to enhance the site. SEO is a strategic process that improves the visibility of a Web page in the search engine results. When a blog article is written, the author can input tag words for the search engines to acknowledge during Internet searches. When more sites link to the specific blog, it increases the search engine ranking for the site. There are many factors that go into SEO configuration. Professional SEO companies are expensive to hire for traditional Websites. Many blog sites appear at the top of the search engines due to the built-in SEO factor.

Blogs can rapidly be shared throughout the Internet like a super fire, which makes them a valuable and popular promotional tool for marketing. There are buttons that allow readers to share a preview of someone else's blog to their social media sites. RSS feed (Really Simple Syndication) is an automatic syndicate of a blog's content where after a blog is published, it goes out to a subscriber's Website, feedreader, or e-mail. Syndication is a free form of publicity that drives exposure throughout the Internet and generates new traffic to the originating site.

There are several blog host sites such as Blogger.com, LiveJournal.com, and WordPress.com. These sites offer a free service to sign up, create a blog, and have the blog hosted on their site. WordPress can integrate a blog into an official Website. There is a "self-host" WordPress account where you sign up only for a user name at WordPress.com. This means you can host the WordPress platform on your own domain site without the limitations that are placed on blogs located at WordPress.com. You still need your own domain name and Web host to use the WordPress platform in a "self-host" capacity.

Once you have a user name from WordPress, you need to login to your Web hosting service provider such as GoDaddy.com and add the Word-Press application to your author's domain name.

Pre-designed templates are available to make it easy to replace the current content with your own. You can search the Internet to locate a WordPress template that meets your needs. There are free templates and premium templates that are available for purchase.

You will need to "add plug-ins" if the template does not contain features such as a RSS feed button for readers to subscribe to your site and social media buttons for sharing your blog. The blog design should allow readers to comment on your published articles for social interaction. There are many "plug-ins" available for WordPress sites.

You can learn how to design and manage a site by going to WordPress.org. The site contains a wealth of information about the platform. If you need further assistant, you can find instructional videos on YouTube.com.

Once the WordPress template is installed on the home page of your official Website, you can start designing the site.

The following list contains sample pages and/or categories to consider for the Website design.

• Home page: This is the main page and used to publish blog articles, news, and updates. An image of the book's cover or advertisement can be linked to the book's sales page. Links to your social media sites where visitors can be taken to your other sites like Facebook and Twitter. The home page can contain any information that you feel is important.

• Bio page: An author's biography and headshot should be present on the bio page.

• Book page: This page should contain a long book description and the book's front cover image. A sample chapter or excerpt is optional.

• Contact page: The publicity, publishing company, and author e-mail addresses should be available on this page for easy contact. You can build a loyal readership by replying to the e-mails as well as build a mailing list of loyal readers.

• Interesting Facts page: Interesting facts about the author or the book's storyline should be included on this page (optional).

• Media page: A digital online press kit with zipped files.

• Blog categories: A blog will help interest people in your book while building a following of readers before your publication date. Your blog articles will be published as a feature on the home page of your Website and permanently stored on the category page. A blog can have various category pages that match the content of the blog articles. When you write a blog, you will designate a category for the content. WordPress will create the category tab for the home page and permanent category page or add the article to a preexisting category page. Publishing a blog frequently will keep your content fresh, and in turn, the new content will help your rankings with the search engines.

After your book is released, there are more promotional pages that can be added to your Website.

• Feedback page: This page should contain quotes from readers and reviewers about what they have said about your book.

• Booksellers page: You should list the worldwide booksellers with links to the book's sales pages.

After your book is published, you can do an Internet search to locate booksellers who have your title for sale to create this list. You can conduct weekly searches for about eight weeks to gather a complete list of booksellers. Some booksellers will take longer than others to list new titles in their inventory.

Many people do searches through search engines or directories. A search engine is a search system that locates relevant information on the Internet in the format of the highest to the lowest ranking. Search results contain information from Web pages and images. A search engine displays results mainly based on relevant keywords located on a Website. A Web directory is an Internet directory that links to Websites by relevant categories based on an entire Website. Web directories list results by the main category and subcategories of the Website.

After your Website is live on the Internet, you can submit your site to the top search engines and directories such as Google, Yahoo, and DMOZ, among others. You can go to SubmitExpress.com for a free Website submission to the top seventy search engines. You can submit your Website to DMOZ directory at DMOZ.org. The Yahoo directory has a free submission for a Website located at Search.Yahoo.com/Info/Submit.html. After the submission process, it can take a few weeks before your information appears in the search engines.

There are Internet blog search engines that strictly search for results on blog sites such as Google Blog Search and Technorati. Tag words are placed on the blog site by the author. These tags and the title of the blog are captured during Internet searches, and the results are ranked by the most recent and relevant blogs with the highest authority scores. Technorati's authority score is a six month popularity rating of the number of unique blogs who have linked to the blog being rated. Other authority scoring is figured by the relevance to popular topics, traffic statistics, and the amount of external blog links. You want your blog's authority to rate high in popularity to gain exposure and new subscribers. After your blog is active, you can sign up and claim your blog site at Technorati.com, which is required for indexing and rating service.

In order for a blog to be included in search engines, the blog site must have a site feed like RSS feed and a pinging service such as Ping-O-Matic or Google Blog Search Pinging. A pinging service is an automatic service that informs multiple search engines when a blog has been updated with new content. If your blog is on a WordPress platform, Ping-O-Matic is used as a default setting unless you manually turn off the service.

Once your Website is built, you can mainly focus on blogging articles and promoting your book for presales. Authors use a blog to build an audience for their book. Will your blog be a personal journal, commentary, or themed articles? A fiction book about vampires could have themed articles about the history, myths, and facts about vampires. The history, myths, and facts are considered different content categories. An instructional book could have how-to articles.

You can brainstorm different subjects for your blog that could be of interest to potential readers. An effective book promotion through blogging is accomplished by satisfying the needs of your readers.

Once you decide on the subject matter, you need to give your blog a relevant name that reflects what the blog is about. This is another technique to get recognized in the search engines during topic searches.

When you write a blog article, you should use the same writing style as your book. This will give you an opportunity to captivate the readers and give them a hint of what to expect from your book. By taking the time to implement the key elements of your unique writing style, you can turn your blog readers into buying customers, increase book sales, and acquire loyal readers.

AFTERWORD

Congratulations, you have acquired essential knowledge about the publishing industry to self-publish like a professional publisher. The next vital step to a successful publishing venture is the book's promotion, which I will help you obtain in my next book, *Book Marketing Like a Pro*.

Book Marketing Like a Pro is a step-by-step guide to develop a promotional plan that will effectively market your book. In *Book Marketing Like a Pro*, we will explore how to promote a book with low-cost marketing techniques that can deliver high-revenue results. The proven methods for obtaining positive sales results involve the following key topics: target market, promotional tools, promotional events, publicity, Internet marketing tools, and Internet promotion.

A strategic, promotional plan is crucial to the success of your publishing company and should be mapped out before you begin the book's promotion. *Book Marketing Like a Pro* will assist you in creating your promotional plan, and you will use this plan as a road map to reach your sales goals.

I wish you much success with your publishing endeavors and your new career as a published author.

APPENDIX

Checklist for Operational Stages

The operational stages will help you get organized and act as a checklist throughout the publishing process. This list provides an overview outline for forming your publishing company to getting your published book in the marketplace.

This entire book should act as a step-by-step guide for the publishing process. If you need more information about a specific task, please refer to the appropriate chapter.

The dollar sign shown at the end of a task means that the task can be an expense for your publishing company. You may have the skills to do the task yourself at no cost to your company or personal resources who can accomplish the task on your behalf.

- Name your company
- Establish a business address $
- Form a legal business entity $
- Acquire licenses and permits $ (not required in all locations)
- Acquire a Federal Identification Number
- Acquire State Sales Tax Permit (only for direct retail sales)
- Open a business checking account (minimum $ to open)
- Open a Paypal business account
- Design a company logo $
- Keep all receipts and log mileage for tax purposes
- Order business stationary, envelopes, address labels, and business cards $
- Identify the book's title
- Acquire ISBN $
- Submit applications to service providers
- Once accepted, look over the contracts, sign and return

- Purchase office supplies $
- Photo shoot for author headshot
- Write book description and author's biography
- Purchase domain names $
- Purchase Web hosting $
- Design Web site and blog
- Set up social media sites
- Request book cover template from service provider
- Book cover design $
- Proof cover design when the file is ready
- Acquire permission for copyright material
- Estimate finished book size and pages
- Set the price for your book
- Set publication date
- Apply for Library of Congress Control Number
- Put manuscript through proofreading process
- Plan the book's structure
- Professional copy editing $
- Apply for P-CIP $
- Interior design $
- Proof interior design when the file is ready
- Set up POD title with service provider $
- POD book proof and shipping fee $
- Proof book and approve if everything is okay
- Start prepublication promotion for presales
- Order POD books $
- Register with the U.S. Copyright Office $
- Apply for library distribution
- Solicit first serial rights

- Register for trade listings

- Submit title for prepublication reviews

- Write and design sales kit materials

- Ship books to Library of Congress, complimentary list, and fill prepublication orders $

- When ready proceed with e-book design layout $

- Acquire ISBN for e-book $

- E-book layout and file format conversions $

- Proof layout and conversion files

- Approve files if everything is okay

- Set up e-book title with service providers

- Proof e-book files from service providers

- Approve e-book files if everything is okay

- When ready proceed with audio book production $

- Acquire ISBN for audio book $

- Proof and approve audio files

- Set up audio book with service providers

- Proof audio files from service providers

- Approve audio files if everything is okay

GLOSSARY

A

Acknowledgement - a thank you by the author to the important people who made a contribution to the book.

Afterword - a final message from an author to the reader.

Appendix - supporting documents and additional material that is not supplied within the book's content.

Audio book - a book that is read by one or more narrators for a consumer to listen to on an audio device.

Author's biography - a summary about an author's accomplishments, qualifications, and expertise that can include published works, educational degree, awards, skills, real life experience, achievements, and membership in key organizations.

B

Back matter - all of the pages that appear after the main story or content of a book such as the appendix, glossary, and index.

Barcode - a scannable code made up of a book's ISBN used by retailers and booksellers to track inventory and sales.

Baseline - the imaginary line the letters sit upon within the text.

Bibliography - cited works for copyright material by another author used within the book's content.

Blog - a personal journal, commentary, or theme articles published on a Web Content Management System (WCMS).

Body of a book - the main content in a book's interior that consists of an author's manuscript.

Body text - the primary text located within the book's interior.

Book description - a brief summary of a book that contains the central idea and main points that support the central idea, or the summary contains the central plot, storyline, and introduces the main characters.

Break-even point - product sales have recovered the initial start-up capital, and the company can begin profiting off of additional sales.

Business entity - the legal structure of a company that involves how it is organized, operated, and the type of taxation.

C

Camera-ready - a file ready for professional printing.

Caption - a brief description of an illustration, graphic item, or photograph used in an interior layout.

Chapter title page - an indication of a break in the story or change of topic within the theme of a book.

Copyright notice - a legal statement that states the book's copyright holder, warning for usage, and how to obtain permission for reprint.

D

Dedication - a thank you to a person or people who have made a difference in the author's life.

Digital rights management - access controls that a publisher sets to prevent the unwanted access to copying, converting, sharing, or distributing the digital content by the consumer.

Disclaimer - a legal statement that pertains to the contents of a book and is meant to protect the publisher and author from legal action arising from the published content.

Distribution - the place books are made available for purchase by consumers.

Distribution channel - an organized process to facilitate the movement of a title from the publisher to distributors, wholesalers, booksellers, and retailers until the product reaches the retail consumer.

E

E-book conversion - a book's computer file that is transferred into various file formats that allow the e-book to be read on specific devices.

Electronic book (e-book) - a digital formatted file that can be downloaded and read on devices such as computers, e-book readers, tablets, and cell phones with Internet capabilities.

Epilogue - a narrative or direct message from an author that brings closure to the characters by wrapping up loose ends beyond the storyline.

External hyperlink - a technique used to link information from within an e-book to outside sources such as Websites, e-mail addresses, and a sales page.

F

Federal Identification Number (FIN) - a nine digit number assigned to a business by the federal government for identification purposes.

First serial rights - the right to publish specific excerpts from a book before the publication date.

Font - a distinctive pattern for capital and lower case letters from A-Z, numbers, punctuation, and special characters.

Font size - the size of text that is measured by numbered point (pt) sizes.

Forced hyphenation - a manual syllable breaking point of a word that is divided with a hyphen.

Foreword - an informative piece about the book's topic and written by a well-known person or a professional, who specializes in the topic field of the book.

Four-step editing process - a process designed for complete focus on specific areas of the manuscript that involves content/story structure, writing and grammar fundamentals, overall effectiveness, and professional copy editing.

Front matter - all of the pages in a book that are located before chapter one begins such as the title page, copyright page, and table of contents.

Full justify - a typesetting technique that aligns the text to be flush against the left and right margin settings to achieve a clean, uniformed appearance.

G

Glossary - a book's dictionary for key terms located within the book's content where words are alphabetized and preceded by the definitions.

I

Index - a quick reference for locating important concepts, terms, topics, and names within a book's content.

Inner blocking - a paragraph formatted by setting new left and right margins to distinguish the paragraph from the primary text.

Intellectual property - a property right that is protected under federal and state law that includes copyrights and trademarks.

Interior design - how the text and layout will appear on the pages of a book and consists of two main elements: typesetting and interior layout.

Interior layout - the arrangement of illustrations, graphics, or photographs in an eye-pleasing balanced environment within a book's interior.

Internal hyperlink - a technique used to link information inside an e-book such as the table of contents, index, and glossary.

International Standard Book Number (ISBN) - a thirteen digit number that identifies the book's title and publisher.

Introduction - an explanation piece written by the author that describes who the book is for, the purpose of the book, and the author's goal for the reader.

Invoice - an itemized document that lists the products billed to a purchaser with the details of all the costs involved with the transaction.

K

Kerning - the individual letter spacing between two letters of a word that appear too loose with gaps or too tight with overlapping.

L

Leading (led-ing) - the vertical spacing between baselines also referred to in word-processing as line spacing.

Left alignment - a typesetting technique that aligns the text flush against the left margin setting to achieve a clean, uniformed appearance on the left side of the page.

Library of Congress Control Number (LCCN) - an identification of a numbering system created for a book's library catalog record and previously referred to as a Library of Congress Card Number.

M

Manuscript editing - a series of edits that locate problematic areas.

Marketing mix - the elements that involve product, price, place, and promotion.

O

Order fulfillment - the process of receiving a product order that includes invoicing, packaging, and shipping.

Orphan - the first line of a paragraph that is left behind at the bottom of a page.

Orphan word - the last word of a paragraph that ends up on the final paragraph line alone.

P

Permission statement - a legal acknowledgement of a copyright holder.

Pinging service - an automatic service that informs multiple search engines when a blog has been updated with new content.

Place - where the product will be made available for purchase by consumers, and the distribution channel of how the product will reach the retail destination.

Preface - a description of why and how the book evolved from an idea into the end product and written by the author.

Premium book - a pre-existing book that is customized for a company's exclusive use as a promotional vehicle to be sold or given away by the company.

Price - an established amount that will be charged for a product.

Print on demand (POD) - a non-inventory model where books are printed to meet the demand of the market.

Product - an item a company will make available for sell in the marketplace.

Product tie-in - a promotional strategy for positioning two products together from different companies in the marketplace to increase awareness and sales.

Prologue - an introductory scene that draws attention to a specific character and event that is presented before the first chapter of a fiction or creative non-fiction book.

Promotion - strategic efforts to reach consumers and inform them about the product for the sole purpose of generating sales.

Publication date - the date a book is made available to the public and often referred to as a release date.

Q

Quantity discount - an incentive offered to a buyer to receive a cheaper price per unit for purchasing a greater quantity of product.

R

Really Simple Syndication (RSS) feed - an automatic syndicate of a blog's content where after a blog is published, it goes out to a subscriber's Website, feed-reader, and e-mail.

Recto - the book's interior pages located on the right side.

Running head - a page header that is positioned above the body text that remains the same layout style throughout the book.

S

Sales kit - an informative packet about a new product that contains sales literature and promotional materials used to acquire new business.

Sans-serif typeface - a font without serif (*See serif typeface*).

Search engine - a search system that locates relevant information on the Internet in the format of the highest ranking to the lowest.

Search Engine Optimization (SEO) - a strategic process that improves the visibility of a Web page in a search engine's search results.

Second serial rights - the right to publish specific excerpts from a book after the publication date.

Self-publisher - an author who takes on the full responsibility of a book's production, distribution, and marketing.

Sell sheet - a sales tool that conveys the most relevant information about a product by using a quick and to-the-point approach.

Serif typeface - a font designed with artistic details at the end of the letters, numbers, punctuation, and special characters.

Social media - Web-based platforms used for global interaction with user-generated content.

Special sales - the opportunity to sell a book in bulk through avenues that do not include booksellers.

Specialty stores - retail stores that specialize in selling theme products.

Start-up capital - a specific amount of money needed to get a business off the ground and product into the market.

Subsidiary rights - parts of a book or an entire book being sold or licensed for a specific use by another party.

Subsidy publisher - a company who charges authors to print books under the publisher's imprint, retains ownership of the author's book, pays low author royalties, and does very little, if any, book promotion.

T

Table of contents (TOC) - a quick reference outline for the contents of a book that consists of chapter numbers, chapter titles, and the page numbers where the chapters begin.

Text justification - an alignment of text between the margin settings.

Title - the professional term used by the publishing industry to refer to a forthcoming or published book.

Tracking - the overall letter spacing between letters within words that creates uniform spacing for groups of words in a headline, sentence, paragraph, and blocked text.

Typesetting - how the type will appear on the interior pages such as the margins, font, size of font, kerning, leading, widows, orphans, and justification.

V

Vanity press - a company who charges authors to publish books and mainly profits from the author fees.

Verso - the book's interior pages located on the left side.

W

Web Content Management System (WCMS) - a Web authoring software that is easy for users without Web design experience to design, manage, and update a blog site.

Web directory - an Internet directory that links to Websites by relevant categories based on an entire Website, and used by Internet users who conduct directory category searches over using a search engine.

Widow - the last line of a paragraph that moves on to the top of the next page and leaves the rest of the paragraph behind on the previous page.

INDEX

CPSIA information can be obtained at www.ICGtesting.com
Printed in the USA
LVOW120857260912

300371LV00001B/3/P

9 780983 327301